AMARUKHAN LODGE

Spirituality, Design, and Setup

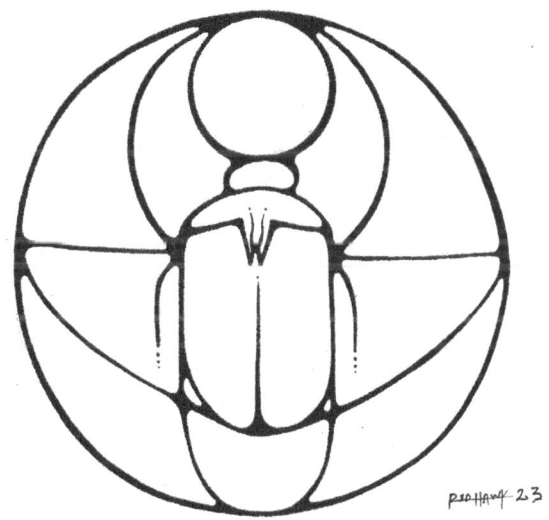

AMARUKHAN LODGE

Written and illustrated by
Eli Jah Redhawk Kenney-Kelley

March 9, 2022
Redhawk
All Rights Reserved

First Edition
Ojai, California
93023

In loving memory of
all the Ancestors of the Original
People who have brought
the sacred light

For
Mama Water Bear
Izes Mosiah I
Savara Mwezi I
Hapi-Heru Hotep I
Nyama Naita-Nwt I
Tanama Atabey Yemaya I
Zemiyah Amaru Kelley

Bless up, giving thanks and izes for all the love
and light you bring
You are my inspiration
Baba loves you

ACKNOWLEDGMENTS

First, I would like to thank Randy Graham of Ojai, California, for seeing this book through and having the heart to help bring this knowledge to the people. I appreciate you; big up!

I would like to give a special thanks to Prophet Neb Naba Lamoussa and the Naba Family in Burkina Faso and Togo, West Africa, for hosting me and bringing me on such a spiritual pilgrimage in the Meritah lands of Kemetic knowledge. Thank you for returning so much knowledge and blessings to the Amarukhan People of Turtle Island.

I would like to thank the Maroon Community Accompong in Saint Elizabeth Parish, Jamaica, for welcoming me and bringing me the truth of bloodline connections between the Caribbean and the Mainland.

Big Up to the Hopi Corn Clan, Chief Ivan, and my brother Vern Makhee in Old Oraibi Village, Arizona, for hosting me and sharing truths of the land, migrations of the people, and the sacred arts.

Bless Up to Chief Stone Coyote for opening my eyes to the depth of our presence on Turtle Island.

So much gratitude and appreciation to Julie Tumamait-Stenslie of the Ventureno Chumash of Ojai, California, for taking me in and giving me the honor of keeping fire for the Bear Dance.

The truth of Our connection with the Land, the Ancestors, and the Divine World can now be restored.

Thank you.

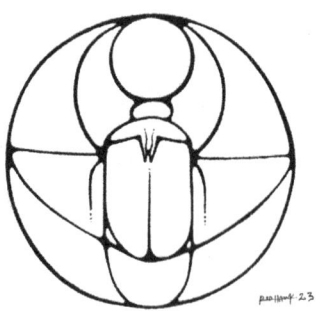

TABLE OF CONTENTS

LIST OF ILLUSTRATIONS
INTRODUCTION
PART ONE: SPIRITUALITY
Chapter 1 - Poles
Chapter 2 - Cover
Chapter 3 - Dew Cloth
Chapter 4 - Door Cover
Chapter 5 - Ropes
Chapter 6 - Lacing Pins
Chapter 7 - Stakes
Chapter 8 - Fireplace
Chapter 9 - Alter
PART TWO: DESIGN
Chapter 10 - Introduction
Chapter 11 - Poles
Chapter 12 - Sacred Measurements
Chapter 13 - Cover
Chapter 14 - Dew Cloth
Chapter 15 - Door Cover
Chapter 16 - Stakes and Lacing Pins
PART THREE: SET UP
Chapter 17 - Introduction
Chapter 18 - Tripod Frame
Chapter 19 - Putting the Cover On
Chapter 20 - Hanging the Dew Cloth
Chapter 21 - Hanging the Door Cover
Chapter 22 - Fireplace
Chapter 23 - Earth Alter
GLOSSARY OF TERMS

LIST OF ILLUSTRATIONS

PART ONE: SPIRITUALITY
Grandmother Lodge
Bird Cover
Bird Tail Lodge
Khepra Design
Khepra Logo
Khepra Lodge Logo
Egg
Sacred Hands
Ankh

PART TWO: DESIGN
10-Foot Pole Horse
Poles
Nine Sacred Body Measurements
Sacred Measurements Full Cover Layout
Sacred Measurements Underside of Cover Layout
Basic Canvas Layout for Cover Pattern
Finished Cover Canvas Layout Pattern
Mapping Out a Cover with Sacred Measurements
Stitches – Basic Cover Pattern
Stitches – Canvas Reinforcements
Stitches – Bottom Edge Smoke Flap Edging and Tie Tapes
Stitches – Top Edge Smoke Flap Edging and Tie Tapes
Stitches – Leather Reinforcements
Canvas Reinforcement Patterns
Cover Hem and Edging
Gores
Lacing Pin Layout
Tying Stone and Cotton Cord Peg Loop
Dew Cloth Panel Design
Door Cover Design
Lacing Pins
Stakes

PART THREE: SET UP
Lodge Frame Ground Plans
Basic Tripod Layout
Tripod Setup
Frame Part 1
Frame Part 2
Frame Part 3
Finished Frame Apex
Rolling Up Cover Bundle
Putting Cover on Frame
Tying Cover Together
Dew Cloth
Door Cover
Fireplace and Earth Alter

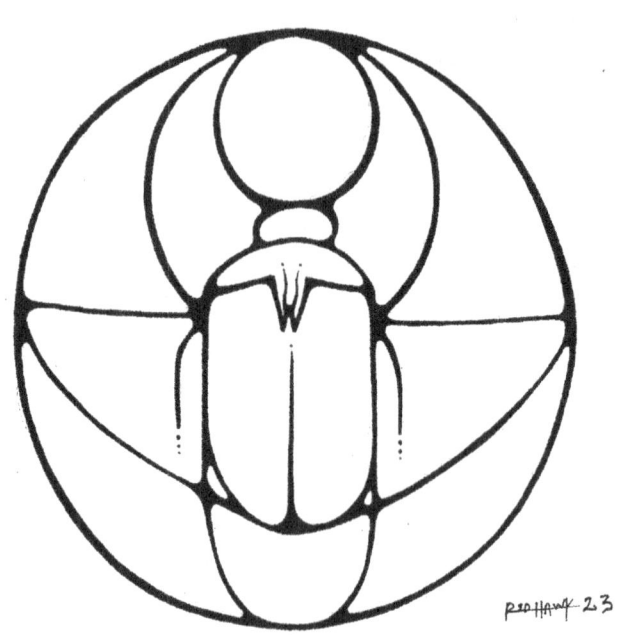

INTRODUCTION

REDHAWK

Udjahee!

Blessings and continual dialectic relations with all our ancestors and those who we are connected with, invisible and visible. We are all here as projections of our ancestral lines, acting as ambassadors for our bloodlines, here to take physical forms. To represent all who have shed blood, sweat, and tears so we can be here now. There is not one aspect of a human being's mental, physical, or emotional body that some relative before us has not carried. In other words, you, as well as everyone else in existence, are not new. We are in continual transformation under the laws of Khepra/god of divine transformation, the being who establishes the order of all existence, so we all may fulfill our purpose, ultimately being an aid and not a block to the becoming.

As Original People we have an obligation to live under the sacred knowledge given to our ancestors by the Neteru/gods and goddesses. The elders say, "You are as good as your father until you prove otherwise." Think of humanity as a tree with all the people connected to the same roots and trunk growing up, branching out into different nations, which branch into different clans, which branch out into different extended families, then branching into the smallest single branches or individual families, with each member a leaf on the branch.

The leaf's purpose is to absorb light and divine knowledge and photosynthesize it into food for the branch or bloodline it is attached to. Thus, it has an obligation to family and the living tree. If the leaf gets pulled from the tree, instantaneously it starts the process of decay. We, too, are not individuals but solely rely on the branch of our ancestral line to fulfill our purpose.

All life derives from Nu/divine fire, Geb/divine matter, Shu/divine air, and Tefnut/divine moisture. Our purpose has to be in accordance with the blueprint the creators of existence set for the Earth and aligned with all the sacred laws that govern the becoming. Our purpose must fill a natural niche within the ecosystem on Earth that supports life for all beings.

To my logic, starting with the basics of our human perspective on the physical dimension at the level of food, water, shelter, and families, there is the greatest imbalance. In the colonial world, these basics are being approached by corrupted, distracted, and abusive minds that disrupt the harmony and stability of existence. We need the original approach again to start to come out of the self-destructive sleep humanity put itself in.

Purpose is fulfilled when a human being is true to their nature and trusting in the intelligence of the Earth. Only then does purpose come like the saying, "When the student is ready, the teacher appears." My purpose was clear when Sacred Grandmother Lodge came into my life.

A timeless Ka/spirit whose origins are mystical, whose story is soul captivating, and who's spiritually powerful enough to continue generation after generation intriguing, touching, and awe-inspiring the genius of the human being while never dimming in her potency. Sacred Grandmother Lodge is star knowledge. Transcending culture, bloodlines, ego, and linear time and space. She even comes from a time before polarity corrupted the human mind before humanity inhabited planet Earth.

There has been no other home or temple as adaptable and universally beneficial to all who experience the beauty, unity with the natural world, and healing properties transmitted by Grandmother Lodge. We are in perilous times, facing the chaos we have created, broken families, and disrupted lifeways. Right now, humanity needs healing that reconnects us to our true nature and purpose. This can only be achieved through the nature-based life that the divine intended for us. I know this is possible for those humble enough to learn the language of the Earth.

Sacred Grandmother Lodge is a channel for Earth and star knowledge, capable of aiding in our healing. Her origins seem very debatable, and everyone has come into contact with Grandmother Lodge from a different source. The truth is there is no "one source" of origin for the Sacred Lodge. She transcends time and space in the form most suitable for the conditions within the ecology of the boundaries of the people who have called her from the stars.

All life is in a continual transformation; Grandmother Lodge is no different. From bark to hide, to canvas, to many styles to express a people, Grandmother keeps coming to the people in the form most suitable for that moment. Sacred Lodge is not something "of the past," or that ends if you kill all the people who have sought her way. She maintains an unshakable purpose that has been handed to me as a continuer of co-creation, manifesting a proper Khat/body in which the Ka of Sacred Lodge can inhabit so she can educate, teach, and remind humanity how to walk with the Earth.

Remember, there is nothing new. All things created from divine intelligence cannot be improved by human genius. Grandmother Lodge comes in different styles and traditions, yet her heart remains the same sacred glow of the oldest ancestral fireplace, and her Ka remains strong. How she functions physically and spiritually remains constant, providing the perfect experience for one to build their Earth relationship that brings a person the qualities our ancestors will be proud of, giving us their blessings as we aid in the becoming.

Existence has harmony and stability it must maintain. We are no different. When we are out of balance, our "being" signals the universe to help us find center. Grandmother Lodge comes to those who have accepted they're here to grow and walk the healing path that maintains the harmony and stability of all life. When you are truly ready to be human, Sacred Grandmother Lodge will find her way into your heart, where you will find your truth once more.

PART ONE: SPIRITUALITY

CHAPTER 1

POLES

The yellow sun makes love with the blue waters of the Earth, and together, they make the green trees that nurture and sustain life. Every tree, along with every other being of life on Earth, is a direct manifestation of the energetic dialogue the Earth is having with other celestial bodies.

Among the Standing People/trees, a tree will tell you when it's ready to become a lodge pole. Called to a tree, we give an offering and prayer for its life and the sacrifice of its place in the forest. We ask the spirit if it will come to help heal the two-legged/humans. Then, we make a cut at the base of the tree. The heartwood remains intact from its base cut to the fine tip at the top. With branches and bark removed, we point the bottom end of the pole so it will grip the Earth for stability in high winds. The pole resembles a double-terminated quartz crystal with the ability to receive and transmit terrestrial and celestial energies. Simply, the lodge pole is an open channel for cosmic dialogue. These open channels are also the path our Ka takes to and from the ancestral plane. On the lodge pole itself, the dark branch knots symbolize the ancestors taking their journeys. Every lodge pole helps open, harmonize, and balance our bodies, hearts, and minds with the Earth. The lodge pole is the path of life.

Here is the story of humanity's original cosmogony: In the beginning, there was only the Nwn, the primordial waters. Ra became aware of himself in the Nwn and created himself outside the Nwn. When he came into being, he saw it was dark and cold. He created Nu/divine fire and Geb/divine matter, so he could have light and warmth, and somewhere to stand. His goal is to bring harmony to existence. Ra looked around and saw that it was good.

Imin became aware of himself inside the Nwn. He created himself to be outside the Nwn. When he came into being, he saw Nu and Geb consuming each other. He created Shu/divine air and Tefnut/divine moisture. He placed Shu and Tefnut in between Nu and Geb. His goal is to bring stability to the harmony Ra created. Imin looked around and saw that it was good.

Ptah became aware of himself in the Nwn. He created himself to be outside of the Nwn. When he came into being, he saw creation moving slowly and that Nu, Geb, Shu, and Tefnut were created… to be continued.

Ra, Imin, and Ptah are known as Neterhent/divine beings too great to be perceived through the limitations of the human being. They are known as the first trinity of Creator Neteru. These divine ones are so great that everything in existence is inside them.

In the Sacred Lodge, Ra, Imin, and Ptah represent three of the four biggest poles selected out of the bundle of lodge poles for the main tripod frame used when setting up Grandmother Lodge. The largest pole of the 4 selected gets put aside for later use. Ra, Imin, and Ptah are the Neteru that created the foundation for existence, they represent the 3 main tripod poles of Grandmother Lodge and are the foundation of her physical existence.

Along with Ra, Imin, and Ptah are the divine ones Knoun, Imsu, and Tem. They are the counterpart Neteru, also of the first trinity of the Neterhent. Knoun, Imsu, and Tem are so small and great that they are inside everything in existence.

We use the clove hitch knot to tie the tripod poles together, which consists of 3 wraps around the apex of the tripod poles and represents "the nature" of Knoun, Imsu, and Tem working with Ra, Imin, and Ptah to get existence ready for its becoming. During setup, the 3 poles put into the lodge frame after the 3 tripod poles are set up, represent Knoun, Imsu, and Tem.

In the setup of the lodge frame, we see how each pole weighs down the previous pole, creating more stability within the frame. The 3 foundational poles to the Lodge's existence represent our life paths and also teach us the order in which we should conduct our lives daily by directing our attention to what's most important. Of the 3 tripod poles, we pick the smallest pole, which represents the self-love that we need to practice every morning so we can be there for ourselves and others. We lay this pole on the Earth. Then, we select the largest pole that represents our family. This pole gets laid on the ground to the right of the previous pole and will eventually rest or weigh down the 2 other poles in the tripod frame.

This pole reminds us family needs to be provided, protected, and cared for before we go out into the world each day. Once ourselves and family have been tended to, then we're ready for work on any given day. Then we select the last pole, the middle-sized pole. This represents our life purpose and work, which is used as the door pole in the tripod frame. When set up, this pole reaches out to become the door pole, creating the doorway for the rest of the poles or community members to join in the circle of life, fulfilling purpose, grounded by self-love and the love of family. This makes for a strong community and base of people working to hold up the goodness of life. That is the tripod.

Cosmogony continued… Ptah looked around and saw that creation was moving slowly, so Ptah took the divine elements and molded all that is. He molded the first two human-like couples, Aishat and Wsr, and Seth and Nebfest. All brothers and sisters in divine human form are immortal but faced with how to play out their immortality in the physical. Seth chose to not share his seed, and with that choice, he sterilized his relationship and is stuck on Earth. Wsr decided to play out his immortality by sharing his seed and going through reincarnation. Aishat and Wsr had a child named Heru. Heru had four sons: Mesthi, Hapi, Duamutef, and Qebsenuf.

Wsr, Aishat, and Heru are our Ancestral Neteru who make up the second trinity composed of Neterwrr/divine beings with humanlike qualities we can identify with. Ra, Imin, Ptah, Knoun, Imsu, Tem, Nu, Geb, Shu, Tefnut, Wsr, Aishat, Heru, Mesthi, Hapi Duamutef, and Qebsenuf tell humanities oldest cosmogony. The 17 lodge poles, which include the 15 frame poles and the 2 outer smoke flap poles, all represent our original creation story from the Nwn to the children of Heru. The children of the children of Heru are human.

While doing Lodge setup, we can always meditate on the original creation story and think about the three foundational concepts that lead to a harmoniously stable life of self-love, family, and purpose. We remember the three types of Neteru: creator and self-created (Ra, Imin, Ptah, Knoun, Imsu, Tem), created by self-created or the divine elements (Nu, Geb, Shu, Tefnut), and divine in human form (Wsr, Aishat, Heru). Like the nature of the tree, the lodge poles continue to live in the community, teaching us how to work together to provide a healing environment to aid in our becoming.

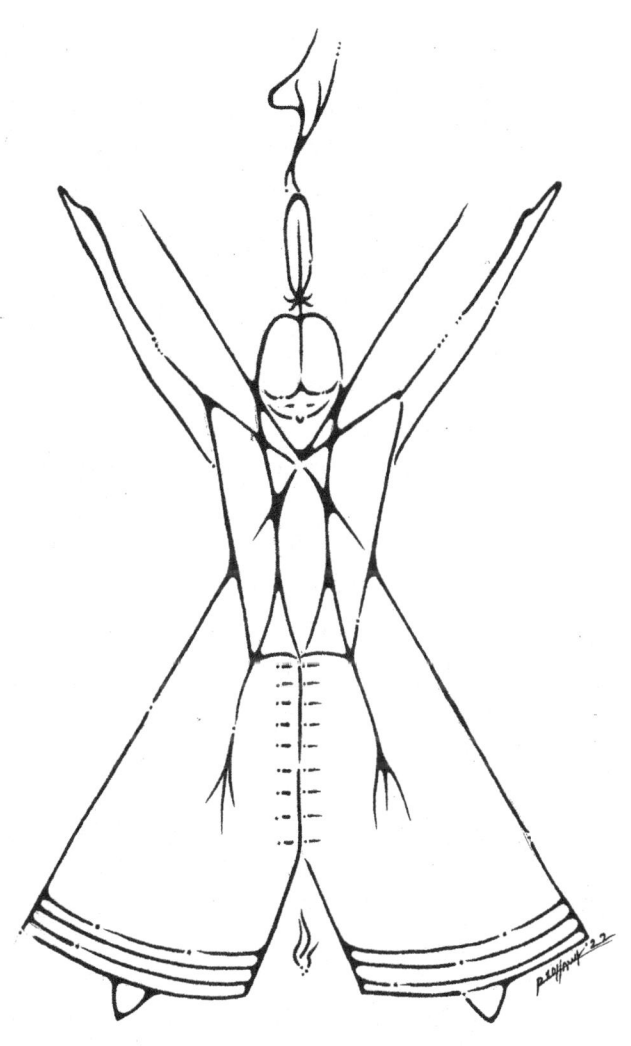

CHAPTER 2

COVER

Existence has no empty space. Diverse groups of intelligence make up the different components of the universe. All these beings, how on Earth can it all possibly work together? One might ask. With no room for "new" ideas in the universe, things simply don't just appear. They become. If it exists, it has a story one can trace back to the beginning of the becoming. This truth reveals that matter doesn't disappear when something dies then the new matter is created upon birth. Matter, as with all existence, is in a continual process of becoming through the cycles of divine transformation.

The Neter/male divinity, Khepra, governs the becoming of existence, having established the laws in which non-material and material realities exist. These laws align every intelligence with its purpose to aid in harmonizing and stabilizing cosmic energies. Anything that breaks the divine laws of Khepra can be disconnected from its purpose. Once an entity loses its purpose, it becomes an obstacle to the becoming. Once an obstacle, that entity enters the cycle of transformation through self-destruction, which ultimately removes blocks in the becoming of existence. It's Khepra's job to make sure existence continues.

If we see Grandmother Lodge as a mini model of existence with the poles representing the Neteru, the foundational intelligence that makes up existence, then we can look at the cover like Khepra and how the laws of the cover determine the path that all other components of the Lodge follow. The cover is fragile. Existence is fragile. If we don't follow the laws of the cover, we could tear it or catch it on fire.

In an instant, existence could be rerouted. However, following the cover's law will shield us from very strong winds, keep us warm below freezing, keep us cool when it is too hot to think, and create an environment worth passing on to our descendants. Like Khepra, the cover determines where the poles find their positions, where the stakes go, where the lacing pins go, how the dew cloth hangs, and most importantly, determines the overall success of the lodge's occupants so they can play their role in the becoming.

The Neter Khepra is shown as a scarab with extended wings holding the Sun and rolling dung in its hind legs. The scarab takes the waste from one being and transforms it into something that benefits life for another. The scarab's body is divided into three main parts that mirror the shape of the human brain, with left and right hemispheres and the frontal lobe. We could ponder, does Khepra represent the logic or mind of existence?

Here is a brief example of the laws of becoming. When I first began my journey in traditional arts, I started by hand-sewing leather medicine bags. As I progressed, I felt a natural calling to learn moccasin making, and I sought to master it. Over time, my skills improved and refined. Then, one day, I was ready to construct a Sacred Lodge. From medicine bags to moccasins to lodges, each step built upon the last, all working together to create a divine transformation.

For the cover of an Amarukhan Lodge, I use canvas 5 feet 3 inches wide. This makes for fewer seams and, ultimately, a cleaner-looking Lodge. I can easily make three generic sizes: a youth 10 foot, a couples 15 foot, and a family 20 foot. I have made Lodges ranging from 5 feet to 26 feet in diameter, and the 15 foot Lodge is by far the best size for it seats 12 people, sleeps 3 to 6, and can be easily pitched by one person. The 15 foot Lodge is made with 3 lengths or strips of canvas. The 3 lengths of canvas represent the Neteru: Aishat, Wsr, and Heru, which are the divine feminine, divine masculine, and divine child in all of us. The canvas strips also represent the 3 components of our being, which allows us to manifest the human experience. The 3 aspects of our being are:

> Ba: Given to us by our Father, this selfless, energetic part of our being has no agenda, the soul.

> Ka: Our complete being without the physical body, the spirit.

> Khat: The physical body to which our Ba and Ka submit too, under the laws or principles that govern its becoming.

Existence follows the laws of Khepra, our unseen aspects follow the laws of matter or our body, and as descendants of the divine here in the physical experience, we too must follow 3 important principles: honoring our ancestors, following the Divine Code of Human Behavior or 77 Commandments, and practicing Zemzem the original form of meditation. The Neteru don't age or get sick. They are pure beings. We, as humans, are fragile and corruptible; we even produce our own waste. We are a threat to the nature of the Neteru. We must work with our ancestors first by raising them to the rank of an ancestor, then disciplining ourselves with the 77 Commandments to keep ourselves spiritually clean. Through learning Zemzem to open and align ourselves through water purification, lamentation, and chants that allow our ancestors to feel safe enough with our presence that they can come close enough to hear our wishes and act as intermediaries bringing our prayers to the divine world when they are unable to help us themselves.

While pitching Lodge, we think about the hierarchy of existence and the order everything must follow to harmonize with the becoming. The smoke flaps on the lodge cover represent the divine beings Heru, who represents good, and his uncle Seth, who represents evil. Both play a vital role in the becoming of existence, and we wouldn't be here without them. The smoke flaps, however, keep the Lodge breathing smoke-free and block the wind, rain, and snow from coming in. Every day one must go outside the Lodge and adjust the smoke flaps to find the perfect balance of openness and protection from the current weather by moving the smoke flaps to be angled downwind and whatever else may be needed for that moment. Every day, we must adjust ourselves to the weather of life to find a balance with the forces of Heru-Seth that are ever-present in ourselves and the world we live in.

When the Lodge cover is ready to go on the frame of poles, we see the established lodge poles in their positions, showing the groups of intelligence that comprise the foundation of existence. The cover wraps around them and instantly establishes the laws governing the path the poles and the entire Lodge will take by the design of the cover, which is Khepra, the Neter of divine transformation. As humans, we are a part of this transformation in the physical world as descendants of the Neteru who are divine in human form, Aishat, Wsr, and their child Heru. The three lengths of canvas that make up the cover represent Aishat, Wsr, and Heru. Sewn together, the lengths of canvas as the complete Lodge cover represent the complete human being as an embodiment of the divine mother, father, and child.

Grandmother Lodge, when properly pitched, is truly a soul-inspiring site that has never stopped keeping me in awe. The smoked cover of an aged lodge against the horizon of the natural world has taught me the wisdom in simplicity and shown me the beauty of the Neteru.

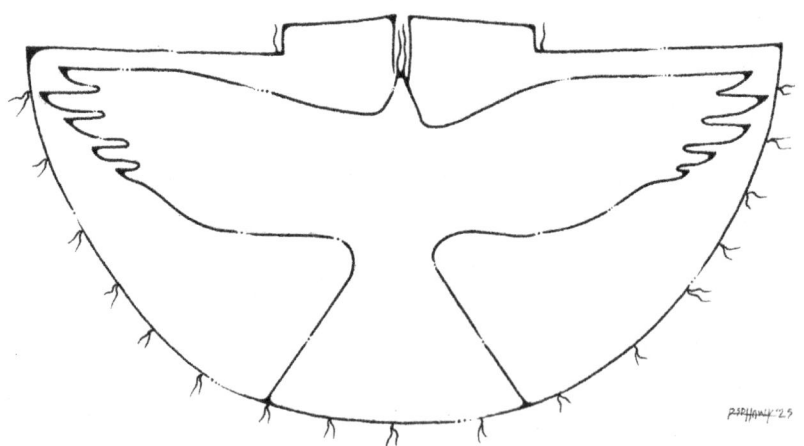

CHAPTER 3

DEW CLOTH

The existence is due to a micro and macro collective of intelligence continuously working toward a harmoniously stable becoming. The becoming is in continual transformation, structured within principles or laws that direct all entities, material and nonmaterial, toward the common goal of existence. As humans, we have an obligation toward existence by honoring the creators and the lineages from them, that allow us to be here now. As humans, we simply cannot invent. We simply replicate what has been exposed to us and can easily be corrupted from all angles. We fight daily with purpose and challenging ambition. Human beings are in a fragile position. Free will allows a human being to "decide" whether or not we "feel" like participating in life today. No other being on Earth applies this "logic," so we need help. The Neteru have given us tools to stay on our path.

Our Ancestors, Zemzem, and the 77 Commandments are the divine gifts we can live by that can create our internal Sa/alter that shields us from the nature of Seth. Within Grandmother Lodge, the dew cloth is hung on a rope strung at heart height from the ground, wrapping around every pole in the Lodge. To this rope, we tie 3 separate canvas panels that hang all around the Lodge and to the ground with a foot length or so laying on the ground either staked down, pinned down by bedding, or stones can also be placed to seal the draft of cool air that gets drawn into the Lodge under the bottom edge of the cover. The cover doesn't touch the ground but is raised slightly above to prevent rot and allow airflow. The dew cloth hangs down along the inside belly of the lodge poles, creating air insulation between the cover and itself. This air space allows fresh air to be drawn under the cover while the heat and smoke rise up and out of the smoke hole above.

The dew cloth creates a warm and cozy space even in freezing weather. With the glow of the fire, the dew cloth also shields the Lodge occupant's shadow from announcing to the camp exactly what is going on inside the Lodge from the shadow shown on the cover outside. As the name implies, the dew cloth keeps excess moisture from settling on your bedding and other belongings in the early morning when it's most wet. It is also the canvas where a person can paint the experiences of one's life. Adding beauty, functionality, and protection, the dew cloth completes the Lodge, creating a sacred healing space where one will forget about time and the outside world.

Each dew cloth panel represents 1 of the 3 most important things for humans to practice creating the dry, insulating, cozy atmosphere inside ourselves that allows the fulfillment of our purpose. Our inner Sa.

We hang the first dew cloth panel from the center of the doorway, going left until it ends. This panel represents the Ancestors and how we relate to them from the physical plane. First of all, not everybody has an Ancestor. We have relatives that pass away and are rebirthed into the Imentet/Ancestral World. They are reborn as helpless as a newborn baby. They need to be fed, cared for, and respected to succeed with strength and life force on their journey in the nonmaterial realm. Once strengthened, the dead relative elevates and becomes an ancestor who can help your destiny.

In the Sidereal Calendar/Original Calander, there are 12 months of 3 Dekans/weeks with 10 days in each Dekan. This 10-day cycle follows the Earth's dialogue with the universe. The fifth day of the Dekan, called ZuDuaNt, it is the day our Ancestral lines come to the Earthly plane to check on their descendants' progression. We have 10 fingers to keep track of this rhythm. This Ancestral Holy Day is the day we offer our Ancestors a small food offering where they feed on the energy and intentions of the meal, thus strengthening their Ka. In return, they help us as intermediaries between our corruptible human existence and the incorruptible pure realm of the Neteru.

Our 7th paternal grandmother gives us our Yen Mialli/prenatal destiny. This grandmother imprints on us conditions that suited her in her last incarnation. Our paternal grandmothers, who are our mother and fathers, fathers, mothers. These are the relatives we call our prayers out to for assistance with our Yen Cabilli/conditional destiny, where we choose the path we walk and reset conditions within the Yen Mialli. These grandmothers can open and close spiritual doors to serve the destiny we create. Our success relies on the approval of our grandmothers. Our Ancestors have approved all the blessings we receive in life. The woman holds power over her children, even after she transitions out of the body.

The next dew cloth panel we hang goes from the center of the doorway, going right till it ends. This panel represents the 77 Commandments given to humanity as a guide to raising our qualities so our Ancestors and Neteru can accept us, and ultimately, we can be clean enough to reenter the Imentet when we make our rebirth from material to nonmaterial to start another cycle of transformation. The 77 Commandments are the root of human spirituality on planet Earth. We received them over 90,000 years ago and follow them today. Here are the first 5 commandments, given to us by the Netert/divine feminine NW, to meditate on:

1 - Thou shall not cause suffering to humans
2 - Thou shall not intrigue by ambition
3 - Thou shall not deprive a poor person of their subsistence

4 - Thou shall not commit acts that are loathed by gods
5 - Thou shall not cause suffering to others

The third dew cloth panel gets hung directly back center of the Lodge and overlaps the other 2 panels on the sides, blocking drafts in the rear bed space. This panel represents the spiritual importance of purifying oneself before attempting to connect with one's ancestors, the divine world, or any spiritual activity. Traditionally, we use ablutions and water purifying practices done before Zemzem, the original meditation given to us by Wsr over 70,000 seasonal cycles ago. In Zemzem, there are positions done to align your being to the Earth and cosmic energies. Then we do lamentations to our ancestors expressing our concerns and wishes. Prayers to the Neteru, chants in sets of 27, and Ka'at ibi/original form of "yoga" practiced in the temples since the beginning of the Phiran/pharaohs. This is where the fountain of Mecca got its name, Zamzam.

If it is understood that we are here to clean ourselves, raising our qualities to be closer to the divine world through the discipline and tools we've been handed down, our ancestral dialectic relationships, spiritual practices, and sacred laws have stood the test of time to reveal our fragility as human beings. Proving humanity needs a divine model to follow because eating, sleeping, and mating are qualities all animals have. The human being has become aware of the divine world, and with our spiritual motivation, we vowed to the divine world we would end our barbaric ways and build our civilization after their example. It is this focus and discipline we will need to continue our becoming and eventually return to continue to assist in the becoming.

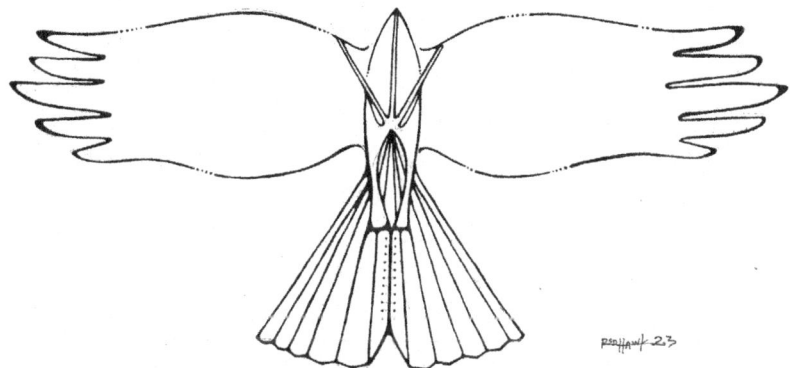

CHAPTER 4

DOOR COVER

Once you have spent many different seasons living in the Sacred Lodge, you will start to understand the various functions of a Lodge and, in time, appreciate the door cover. There will be extremely hot days where you roll the door cover up and unpin the cover, opening the whole front for a breeze. On rainy days, when the door cover receives buckets of rain, you're glad it's there. Those windy moments when you have to tie the door cover down to the stakes, hoping it doesn't come undone and blow dust into the Lodge. Snowy nights when you need your fire going well, but the snow has blocked all airflow around the edge of the cover, so you prop up the door cover with a stick, so the doorway becomes the source of fresh air in the Lodge. The door cover is constantly adjusting and readjusting. Even if you have to go somewhere, a well-tied door cover prevents larger animals like dogs, bears, and deer from just making themselves at home while you are away. Over time, one finds the door cover is adjusted as much as the smoke flaps above and is spiritually a strong symbol of protection.

To understand the human situation, one must know the nature of evil. Immortality is its character, ever-present and seeking a fresh pasture. Evil can manifest in the criminal, victim, and witness all at the same time, never hesitating to show up when you least expect it. To lure you, it usually comes in the forms of distraction and pleasure, knowing all too well the fragile nature of the human being. For the human being, the mind is Seth's doorway to our hearts, making us vulnerable yet aware that we must have clean bodies, minds, and hearts to stay balanced, thus creating a shield against evil. The greatest tool to protect ourselves from the storms is simply our prayers.

One may ask, why do human beings need to pray? Our ancestors have set the conditions or general guidelines for their descendants to live by. The descendants are just one aspect of the ancestral lineage being projected on Earth with the goal of preserving the bloodline by raising its qualities. Like the leaf on a branch, we are not separate from our source. We're so connected to our ancestors that we cannot progress without the approval of our maternal and paternal great-grandmothers, who carry the power over our destiny. The only way one fulfills purpose is through the dialectic relationship we have with our ancestors. Prayer is our survival.

Belief is based on emotion; emotion cripples our logic. There are times to reach our ancestors while feeling emotional but remember that prayer is most effective when one feels grounded in the body, heart, and mind. The prayer should be based on what we know. What we know is remembered by the heart. Pray with your heart. It will be answered.

The door cover symbolizes protection, coming as a result of our prayers being answered. Our prayers are directed to the women who have the spiritual power over our bloodlines, so we think about our ancestors who have shed blood, sweat, and tears every time we move the door cover aside to go in or out of the Lodge. These women made it possible to be here now, and it's their approval that gives us permission to move from the nonmaterial to material worlds, like going from outside the Lodge to stepping inside. The whole environment inside has an established order within a much more confined reality like the human experience compared to the dimension of the ancestors. We always know the time spent in Grandmother Lodge is temporary, like our time in the human experience, where before we know it, we must return to the outside world where most of our experience takes place.

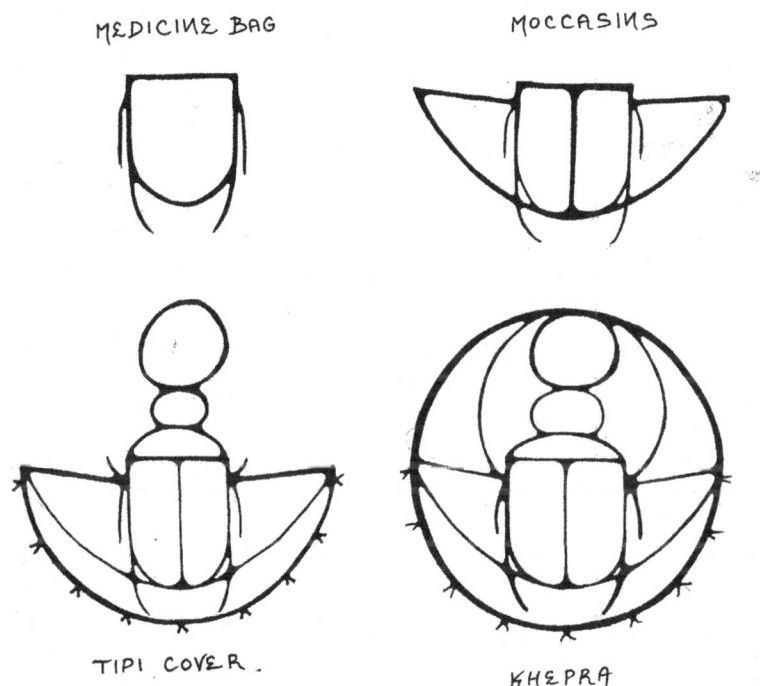

CHAPTER 5

ROPES

Earth is in a continual dialogue with the universe. Every component or entity within the universe is in an energetic dialogue between Earth and all other celestial bodies. We get the concept of 24 hours in a cycle of day and night from the reality that the Earth transmits from its core energy out through every component 24 times in a day and night cycle. This transmission from Earth is the Earth responding to energy projected toward it from other celestial bodies.

This dialogue between the Earth and the cosmos creates channels of energetic flow that create harmony for the Earth. Life on Earth is the consequence of this harmony being made. This harmony demands every intelligence that composes everything on Earth's material and spiritual bodies to stay in a continual adaptive nature to keep these energetic channels open, maintaining harmony for existence. The energy a celestial body emits toward Earth is called Yennu. In response to the authoritative nature of Yennu, the Earth responds with a reaction from the heart or core by sending out its energetic makeup or spiritual identity to the rest of the universe. From stones to elephants, everything on Earth is a part of this spiritual identity.

Under the laws of Yennu, this spiritual fluid of energy inhabits matter to create lifeforms as one of its expressions. The response nature of spiritual identity fluid within all bodies demands that a being's behavior is within the harmony of this cosmic dialogue. The physical body could be seen as the instrument that transmits the Earth's heart energy toward the cosmos and functions to adjust and readjust the Earth's energetic identity to stay in harmony with existence. The energy emitted from Earth through the life on it toward other celestial bodies also gives us the perception of our manifestations as our interior psychological space.

This spiritual fluid is called Bayuali. It is birthed, channeled, and then fades out by its nature, making no material manifestation on Earth permanent as it continues to its next stage of becoming. When a being's behavior doesn't align with the cosmic harmony, one cuts the Bayuali connection from the Earth, putting oneself into a state of psychological disconnect from nature and is rejected by nature as that being enters a self-destructive space that is designed to remove that obstacle from the harmony of the Earth's becoming.

Cosmic dialogue is essential for maintaining harmony and stability for the universe and the becoming it is in. Life is a manifestation of this dialogue and is thus designed to adapt and readapt to its behavior to stay an open, connected channel for Earth heart transmissions. Yennu, Bayuali, and life create a sacred electrical rope, allowing the universe to function and remain intact. This principle is directly related to the frame rope of Grandmother Lodge, its design, and its purpose. The frame rope of Grandmother Lodge is made of 3 bundles of plant fibers twisted together to create the component that holds Grandmother Lodge together so she can function and continue her becoming. The rope wrapped around the apex of the lodge poles usually has enough left over after the initial wraps to hang to the ground in the back of a Lodge. It can either be wrapped down a tripod pole or staked down in the Earth, reinforcing the whole Lodge for high winds.

There is no Lodge without ropes. They are the lifeline for the proper function of the Lodge. So, too, the energetic channels of planetary dialogues are held as the ropes holding life and existence together. The yellow Yennu of the sun makes love to the blue Bayuali waters of Earth. Together, their children are the green plants that nourish nature and sustain all life on Earth.

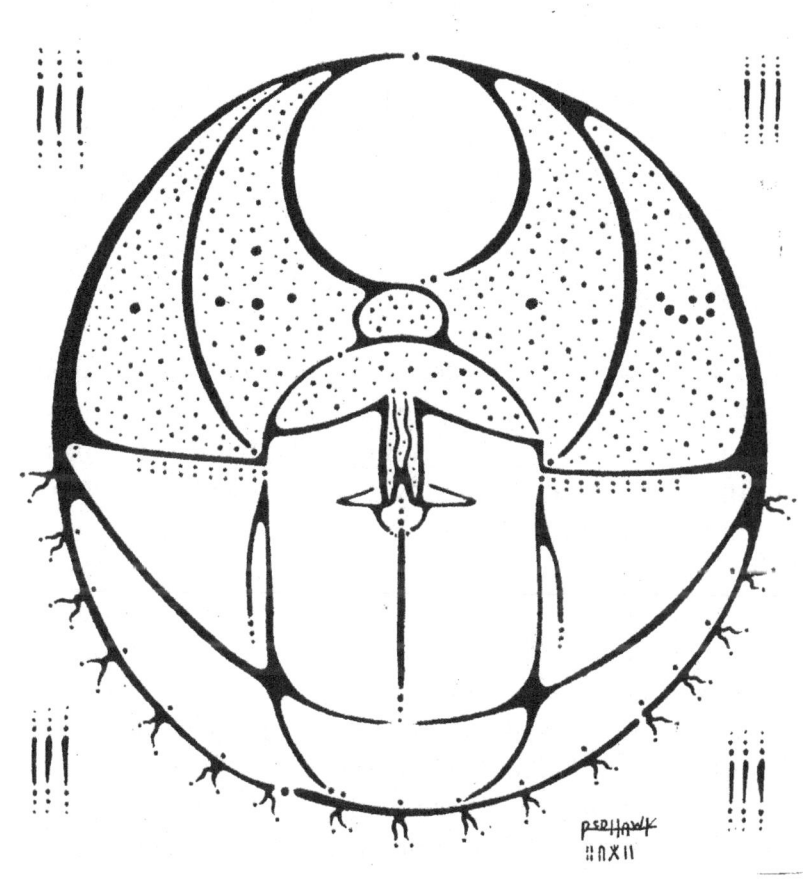

CHAPTER 6

LACING PINS

How do we track time as human beings on the Earth with a limited perception of the senses and disadvantaged by our limited size? The completion of a celestial cycle determines time. Furthermore, a celestial cycle is determined by viewing a celestial body rise above the eastern horizon and pinpointing the exact location on the horizon where the celestial body rose. A cycle is complete only when that celestial body rises exactly on that point again.

From the Earth's perspective, human beings must rely on the cycles of celestial bodies to know our appropriate place in time and space. For as long as humanity has observed celestial phenomena, humanity has witnessed a cycle that has proven for over 54,000 years to be the only precisely accurate cycle. This is the Sidereal Cycle between the Earth, Sun, and Sirius star. The accuracy of the Sidereal Cycle is the only cycle consistent every time that is worthy to have a calendar based on it. 365 days is a seasonal cycle from rainy season to rainy season. 365 days is not a year based on a consistent cycle between the Earth and Sun or Earth and Moon. It takes 56 seasonal cycles for the Sun to complete a cycle with the Earth, and 18 seasonal cycles to complete a full cycle with the Moon. Earth's rotation, speed, and wobble are too inconsistent to make a calendar.

Every 1,460 seasonal cycles from the Earth's perspective, the Sun eclipses the dialogue or energies between the Earth and the Sirius star system. This creates a great disruption to the harmony of the Earth and takes Earth one seasonal cycle to regain its stability and renew itself. The human body doesn't last 1,460 years to base a calendar on it. However, when we consider a seasonal cycle of 365 days long, this smaller cycle is what is the foundation of the calendar of humanity. We take 1,460 seasonal cycles between these celestial phenomena and add the 1 seasonal cycle for Earth's renewal, we get 1,461 seasonal cycles to a "great year." Divide 1,461 by 4 and get 365¼. Each day represents 1 seasonal cycle in the great year in the sidereal eclipse cycle. 4 seasonal cycles on Earth of 365 days are 1,460 days. Every four seasonal cycles, we add the extra Earth renewal day to the calendar, making the "small year" 1,461 days long. Each quarter of a small year is 12 months long.

There are 5 days at the end of each 12 month cycle, which are the birthdays of Neteru Heru, Aishat, Wsr, Seth, and Nebfest. This makes 1 seasonal cycle 365 days long. Adding the 1 extra day on the Sidereal Calander every 4 seasonal cycles represents the seasonal cycle after the solar eclipse that the Earth renews itself. This also shows why the colonized mind claims the "year" is 365¼ days long and calls the sacred Earth renewal period the "leap year." Each month on the Sidereal Calendar is 3 dekans long. Each dekan is 10 days long. This 10 day cycle is based on the Earth's dialectic communication with celestial bodies, determining the appropriate energies and moments for proper spiritual activities. This cycle of a 10 day rhythm is why we can count it on our hands. Each of these 10 days is named and has a specific role in how we interact with the divine and ancestral realms. The Sidereal Calendar has been in use for over 54,000 seasonal cycles.

One might say that cycles of time are like the lacing pins on the Sacred Lodge. Each one is a stitch that holds together our existence. The 10 lacing pins on the front of the Lodge represent the 10 Heru or "days" of a Dekan or week and can be used to track this sacred Earth rhythm by hanging cloth to mark the day, starting from the bottom pin moving up a pin a day.

Days 1 to 3 of the Dekan are for water purification and Zemzem. Day 4 is a day of rest to clean the temple space. Day 5 is Ancestral Holy Day, in which we cook a meal for our ancestors. Days 6 through 8 are for water purification and Zemzem. Day 9 is Divine Holy Day, in which we offer frankincense and prayers to the divine world through the channel of our Ancestors. Day 10 is the second day of rest to clean temples and prepare for a new Dekan.

The knowledge of our place in time and space determines, like lacing pins, whether we, too, stitch and hold together the fabric of existence.

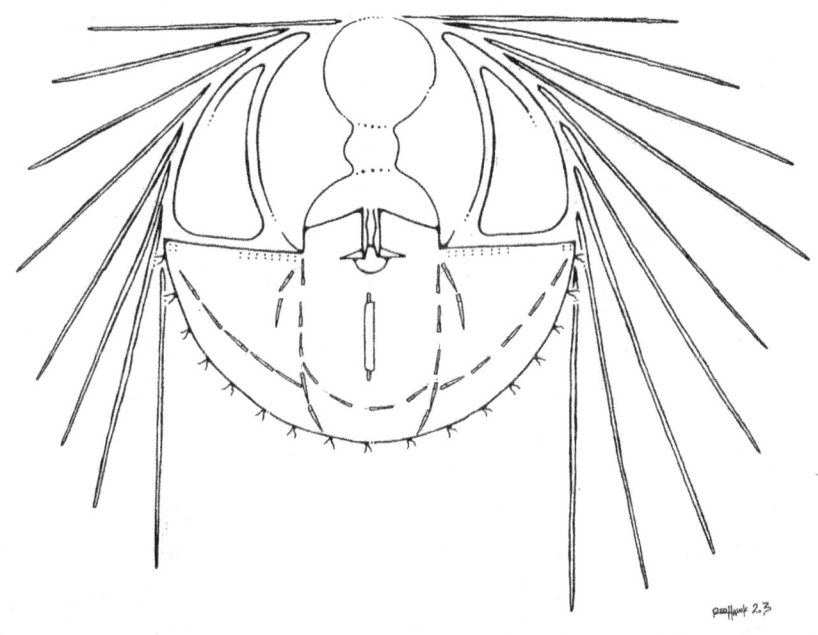

CHAPTER 7

STAKES

In the original initiation schools, the priests teach a concept of the world as an egg model. See the world as an egg in which all of its components work together toward the common goal of harmonizing and stabilizing the becoming of the egg. This "world" is an egg concept called a Zouhet, where the shell, whites, yolk, blood, membranes, and every other component of the egg have the common goal of preserving this stage of the becoming of the egg.

The Priest teaches us the world of a Zouhet is a contained group of intelligence in a particular dimension of time and space, allowing existence to evolve under the authority of the destiny of the Zouhet. Every Zouhet is composed of selected groups of intelligence, actions, reactions, and consequences, each with its destiny. Each destiny creates a separation between every Zouhet, yet every Zouhet is linked to all others. This multiple Zouhet reality means that when one transitions or dies, there are many more Zouhets that reharmonize and continue the becoming of the world. This creates harmony and stability for existence. Otherwise, if there was only one Zouhet that made up existence, any failure of one of its components or intelligence could destroy the whole. Every Zouhet is a dimension of time and space and can only be perceived from the outside.

When pitching Grandmother Lodge, it is at the step of staking down the cover the Zouhet teaching comes to mind. A properly staked Lodge, from a bird's eye view, looks like an egg, oval with a narrow end toward the doorway and the widest end making the open, roomy back of the Lodge. Each stake can be seen as an intelligence working for the stability and harmony of the egg. The stakes can also be viewed as individual Zouhets linked together to make a bigger Zouhet, the Sacred Lodge. If one stake pulls out in a strong wind, there are still many more that can be reconfigured to maintain the destiny of the Lodge. When I stake down Grandmother Lodge, with each stake, I think about a Zouhet or world which I'm connected with, like a particular ritual that helps keep my life from an energetic collapse. Understanding all dimensions, realities, and worlds as interlinked Zouhets that shape and build every step in our becoming.

Grandmother Lodge is a Zouhet, a world in which many entities evolve within a designated time and space according to the energetic dialogue between all her components: the standing people or poles, stone people, fire, Earth, wind, water, plant people, humans, and all nonmaterial entities inhabiting Grandmother Lodge. She is a living, breathing world of her own becoming that we can become a component of and work toward the harmony and stability of the energetic dialogue between ourselves and the Earth linking us to the becoming of Grandmother Lodge. The Lodge gives us an accurate perspective of our place in time and space. Grandmother Lodge is a world all her own, closer to the Neteru.

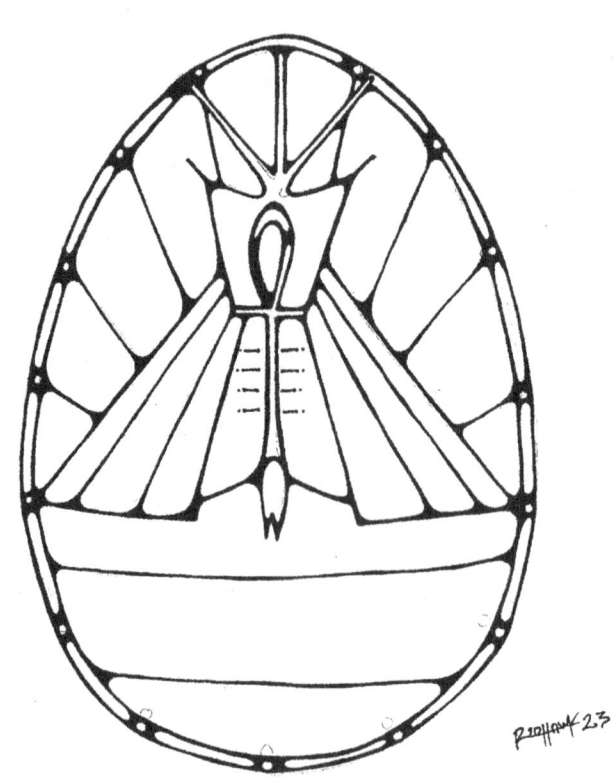

CHAPTER 8

FIREPLACE

Every physical body that a soul inhabits produces its own body heat. We all carry an internal fire that requires constant tending and feeding. This fire's light is the source of divine knowledge and understanding inside ourselves, and its warmth is shared with all when we live from our hearts. It is the presence of life that brings the warmth, and warmth that brings life.

The Ka is the energy and identity of all earthly forms, and on the molecular level, the Ka is the very component that bonds molecules so matter can stick together and create forms. The Ka alone is a pure entity free from material corruption. However, a Ka inhabiting form or matter is subject to the becoming of the matter. Matter carries corruption from our thoughts, hearts, environmental toxins, and waste-producing systems. Our body is a danger to the purity of the divine. That is why they gave us the 77 Commandments or Divine Code of Human Behaviors, along with ablutions or water purification rituals to help us humans keep our minds, bodies, and souls as clean as possible. The nature of fire is to destroy the corruption of matter and allow the Ka to be free from matter's imposing nature. In other words, fire purifies through its destructive nature; as fire burns matter, the Ka is released. Ka is absorbed by other entities that can benefit from an energetic charge.

The central fire of Grandmother Lodge is the most important component. When a person experiences a small blazing fire, one will feel the Lodge inhale cool air under the bottom of the cover, coming in to refresh the Lodge and exhaling all the smoke and stale air out of the smoke hole.

While gazing up, one witnesses the expanse of the cosmos in the night. Then, the person is drawn outside to see the expanse of the sky. Outside, the person leans on the Lodge, illuminated and glowing, as to invoke the Ancestors and to come and enjoy the warmth emanating from the canvas cover. Only then does one realize the fire is Grandmother's heart, giving her breath and awakening her to share warmth and knowledge with those who are willing to listen and receive.

The fireplace holds the keys to cosmic consciousness. We cannot perceive the elements in their divine form, meaning every element is a mixture of all the elements in different ratios, so it is hard to perceive fire without matter, air, and water. Fire in the divine form is the Netert Nu. Nu is responsible for giving humanity almost half of the Original 77 Divine Laws. A guide for mind, body, and soul to keep as pure as humanly possible to preserve life and accept, not reject, the dialogue of existence.

Remember the great Neter Ra, who created himself from the primordial waters of the Nwn. Ra created Nu and Geb to have warmth and light and a place to stand. Nu is female, Geb is male. In Lodge, we see the central fireplace of a ring of stones and the fire inside as Geb and Nu bring harmony into existence. The ring of stones represents man and his duty to create a circle of protection around the feminine. A man without a woman can become hard and cold, hurting all. The fire represents a woman with her ability to give and take life, and with such power, if she doesn't have a ring of protection around her, she can't feel safe enough to shine as brightly as she is. In this unsafe space, her power can lose control, and she can hurt herself and others. Proverb: "A ring of stones without a fire leaves them cold and hard. A fire without a ring of stones can burn down the village. Together, peace and harmony rule the Lodge."

The nature of the masculine and feminine union creates the foundation for what we call the Trinity. This union creates life, creating a family. Healthy families create healthy communities. Healthy communities create healthy nations. Healthy nations create a healthy world. It's up to us to contain, feed, and tend our inner sacred fires so we all help to illuminate this beautiful Earth, and family is an excellent place to start. After all, what good is a Lodge fire without family and friends?

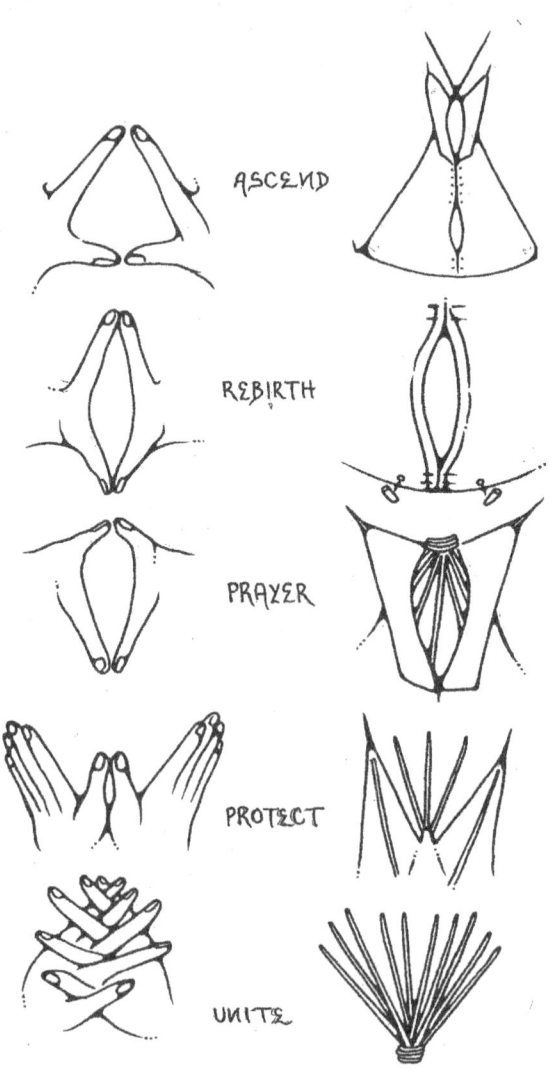

CHAPTER 9

ALTER

One's success in life is based on several obvious yet often overlooked factors of the human experience. Success can mean something different to every person. However, what the human being determines is success through the mental process, usually based on societal programming. Our view of success generally is out of one's view because we have cut off half of our experience by putting what happens in the material realm above or separate from the realms of the unseen. We now generally don't consider the reality that for "anything" to exist in the material realm, it is already unseen energy or a select group of intelligence awaiting its passage through a channel that will bond spirit and matter. There is no material form without its energetic identity, which matter uses as a blueprint to build the form.

For the human being to achieve, success is based on the approval of our bloodline mothers, who are responsible for opening or closing the spiritual doors of our destiny. If your Mama is not happy with you, your chances of success are limited because it was her Ka that inhabited your body while in her womb and infused your being with her creator power. You owe her everything. She gave your bloodline another opportunity to refine, purify, and move the family forward as the person who is representing all that have come before. To obtain success, one has to have strong relationships with whatever we require as an ally to achieve our goals.

To have a relationship with our deceased grandmothers, one has to establish a space. How you only cook in the kitchen, not the bathroom, everything requires its designated area where the natural, spiritual factors of a concept have the room to be manipulated and focused on, to allow its manifestation. The Jengili/Ancestral Stone Alter creates the space to achieve the spiritual success that will manifest one's success in the physical experience. Nature demands a constant adjusting of energies to stay balanced and harmonized with the universe. Maintaining life is the goal. Success is based simply on whether or not your thoughts, words, and actions preserved life, or took it at the end of the day.

Success is not the manifestation of your ego and is not based on what you think. Instead on whether the Earth accepts or rejects your energy. See it this way: if you need shelter, food, and water to maintain success in the physical, you need a space that is pure enough that your ancestors won't get hurt from our corruptions and are willing to connect with you. First, by feeling safe enough, then entering and building a dialectic relationship with you so that, if nothing more, they are pleased you're in gratitude for what they've given you.

The Jengili is the most important place one establishes to maintain their spiritual connection to creation. First, a human being has to purify oneself before establishing such a space. The Jengili is the channel in which the Bayuali, or transmissions of Earth energies, and Yennu, or transmissions of celestial energies, have the opportunity to harmonize without blockages created by the mind. Preventing the Earth from relating to its sources of origin, its mother, through its energetic dialogue with the universe. There would be no Earth if the universe saw it as an obstacle to its becoming.

A stone comprises very few groups of intelligence, creating a very slow becoming for the stone and allowing the physical body of a stone to last millions of seasonal cycles. A human is comprised of many intelligence groups, thus creating a much faster becoming due to the increase of energy input required to maintain these groups of intelligence. Resulting in our bodies wearing out comparatively quickly with the rest of the natural world. Stones are then the best transmitters of the Earth's spiritual identity. Our ancestors knew this and thus used stones as tools within the pure space of the Jengili to open the channel that allows access to the memory of the Earth. It is at the Jengili that human beings maintain their energetic relationship with the cosmos. All our ancestors are accessible through the Jengili, and anybody disconnected from their spiritual origins is like a leaf pulled off the branch. It will instantly start to wither and lose its life force. You might say the Jengili is the umbilical cord that connects us to our life source and, ultimately, our creators.

So important is the stone altar that Greco-Romans tried to copy the models they saw in Kemet. After studying in the temples, they hired priests to establish replica sites in Europe. Places like Stonehenge are presented as mysterious. This is simply because, as a "civilized" person on a mission to progress, you are not allowed to know the world's original spiritual influences. Anything deemed a "mystery" is my story, and for the modern colonial world, that means its origin is kept secret like the word "origin," which backward is "nigiro".

The altar, located within the sacred space of Grandmother Lodge, allows the Grandmother to engage in dialogue with creation. The inhabitants of Grandmother Lodge become a part of her being that supports the maintenance of life on Earth.

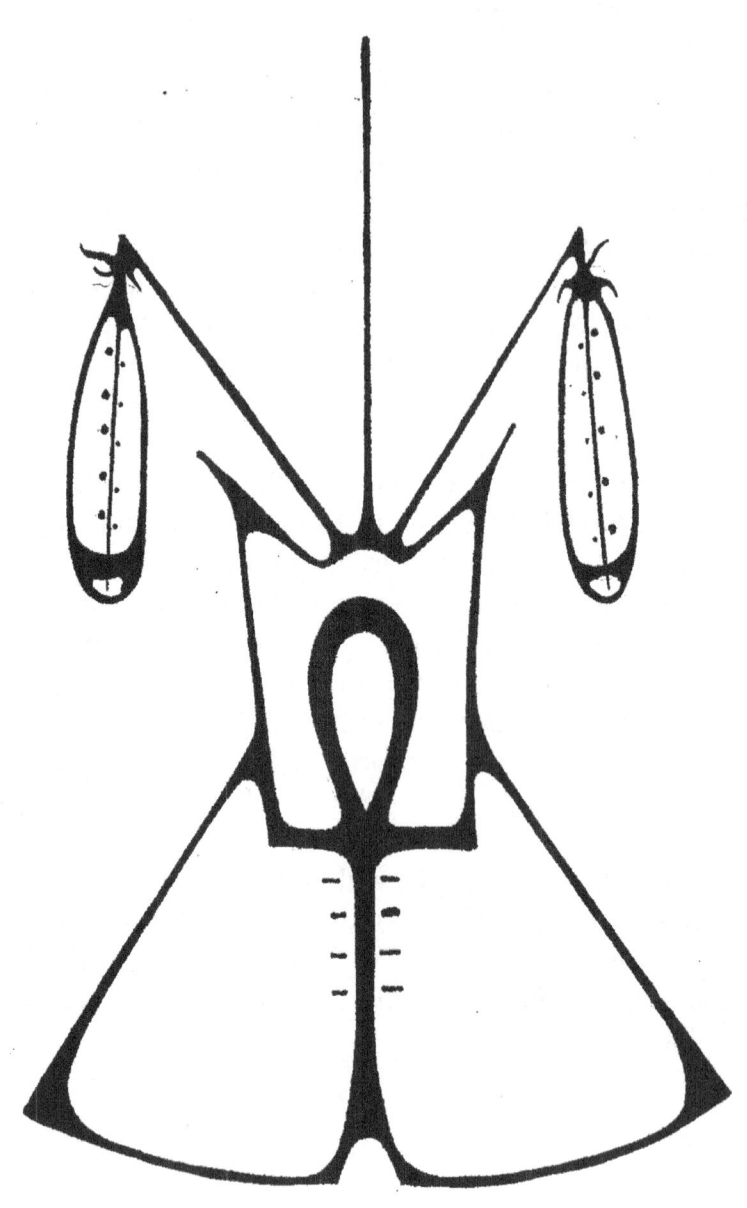

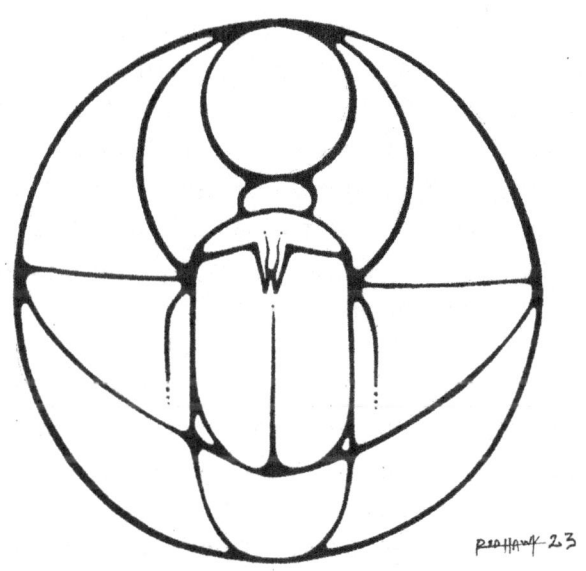

PART TWO: DESIGN

CHAPTER 10

INTRODUCTION

We start this section on Lodge design by acknowledging the ancestors who have led me to the doors containing sacred knowledge, understanding, guidance, wisdom, and patience to bring this book to light. Duaoo/thank you, relatives, to my left and my right, showing us the knowledge we seek is already inside our body temples. This internal knowledge allows us to manifest the temple of the Sacred Lodge, which provides the external environment necessary for healing. For this, we are forever grateful, humbled, and in your service. May we continue to build our relations so they never break again.

Living in the Lodge for over seven complete seasonal cycles has given me the experience needed to deeply understand all functions of the Lodge and the creative drive to design a unique style that meets the needs of an artistic eye. The Amarukhan Lodge is not a copy of another nation's Lodge style but an addition to the list of over forty tribal types. I have stayed true to the key characteristics of traditional canvas lodges to bring a true Sacred Lodge experience to all. No one, however, can improve the original tried and true designs, yet all nations add their unique color and spirit to Sacred Grandmother Lodge.

As we go through the design process, I'll highlight the features that make the Amarukhan Lodge unique. I can say that what makes the design of the Amarukhan Lodge truly unique is that it was designed from the Nine Sacred Measurements of the human body. This approach to custom design provides a home and temple that truly fits its owner's mind, body, and spirit like a new pair of shoes made for you. When a Lodge is designed this way, a person will connect with the experience on a profoundly deep level and gain new respect for the divine architecture of all things natural.

I'm not here to make replicas, I'm here to ride the tides of divine transformation through adjustment and readjustment. All living things experience this process. Grandmother Lodge is no different. The Amarukhan Lodge is a continuation of this sacred healing path, aiming to bring Lodges into the light of the new dawn. Remember, what is built on falsehoods dies because it can't grow roots. What's built on truth outlasts all who were there to see its birth.

CHAPTER 11

POLES

You'll need the following tools: a 30 inch bow saw, sharp hatchet, drawknife, and 10 foot pole horse, which I show how to construct in the illustration.

Materials you'll need: Depending on your body height, you will choose one of these two pole options.

Body Height	# of Poles
4 - 5ft	17
6 - 7ft	21

Early spring is the time to harvest a fresh set of poles. After all the rain and snow of winter, the forest, specifically the trees, is full of water, making peeling the bark off a fresh lodgepole very easy. The spring temperatures also make a very suitable "warm but not too hot" environment to cure or dry a set of poles.

The type of trees available differs significantly from region to region. The most preferred Lodge poles have been Lodgepole Pine and Yellow Pine, Red Cedar, and Firs like Western Douglas Fir and White Fir. The term lodgepole refers to growing conditions in the forest where a thick grove of young trees compete for the light, ultimately growing arrow-straight and very thin compared to its height. These trees will usually not make it to full maturity in the forest due to the "lodgepole" growing conditions. By selecting a set of poles with awareness of the surrounding trees and the overall condition of that area, one can increase mature tree success by decreasing competition for soil, light, and water.

Selecting poles in the forest is a pure meditation, tuning a person into tree awareness. Once you feel called to a tree and you feel it's tall and straight enough from all sides, there's one more measurement needed to determine if the tree can become a lodge pole. The width of the largest lodge pole in a bundle will be no wider at its base than the widest part of an open palm of the hand. Walk up to the tree and put your hand on it at the level of your heart to see if the tree is as wide as your palm. If it's more than a thumb width wider or a thumb width smaller, then select a different tree. The right tree will be about your palm's width at your heart height with the bark on, however, all the poles will be slightly different sizes. Also, remember you need all but 2 poles in your bundle to be strong, sturdy frame poles, leaving the last 2 poles for the smoke flap poles. These poles are always selected a bit thinner than the frame poles for their needed flexibility.

Step #1 - Depending on your body height, which you multiply by 4 to get the specific length for your lodge poles, you will need either 17 or 21 poles. Get a scrap of red fabric and cut it into 17 or 21 strips. These strips of cloth will be used to tag your selected trees in the forest. You can quickly relocate your poles by tying the strips at eye level around each trunk after locating each suitable tree.

Step #2 - Using either the bow saw or the hatchet, or both, fell the trees as close to the ground as possible. Even if the bottom couple of feet of the tree is too big or crooked, so as not to leave an unfinished job of forest management. Starting at the top or small end of the tree that you just cut, use the width of your thumbnail, find where your thumbnail is the same width as the wood, and cut off the tip. This removes just enough weak wood at the end of the pole so that the final pole will be suitable for transportation and less likely to break or get snagged if it falls over.

Step #3 - At this point, starting at the fresh cut-off tip of the pole, measure out the length you need from the top end of the pole going down toward the base. Cut to the proper length, which should be your body height multiplied by 4. A person 6 feet tall needs lodge poles 24 feet in length.

Step #4 - We have the pole in its final length, and now we need to use the hatchet, making sure it's as sharp as possible, to cut the branches off the pole. Start at the butt or bottom of the pole and cut off the limbs, always swinging toward the pole's tip, which is with the grain of the wood. This is a delicate step. One must cut the branches off and try to bring the knobs of the branches down to the level of the tree trunk without excess gouging into the main pole or removing too much wood to create more unlevel surfaces. Also, at this point, the bark is still on the tree, and you won't be able to do the full deknobbing required until after the bark is completely peeled off. You will want to do all the delimbing right there on the site you cut the tree down. Once de-limbed and cut to length, it's ready for peeling.

Step #5 - This is the step where we use the pole horse made from the diagram provided or find two trees with about ten feet between them, making sure each has a fork or branch at least waist height so a lodge pole can be laid level in the crotches creating a good workstation. Two regular saw-horses can also be used for a pole workstation, but one must add two blocks of wood four inches apart on the top middle of each saw-horse to create a channel for the poles to lay in so it doesn't roll off the horse. Once a good workstation is established, it's time to peel the poles.

Step #6 - The sooner you peel your fresh-cut poles, the better. Waiting too long will result in a dried bark being much more challenging to peel. I suggest at least getting started the day of cutting or the next day so the bark is so moist that your hands can even peel it. Start at the butt end of the pole to be peeled. Using a drawknife, peel the pole up the grain, bottom to the top of the tree. When you reach a knob that needs to be leveled, work it gently with the drawknife until it is completely level. If it's a very big branch knot, try to work it the best you can and continue peeling the pole. When all the poles are peeled, go back over the entire bundle and finish smoothing all knobs and anything along the pole that could tear the canvas or create a point for water to drip into the Lodge in a storm. The proper lodge pole is your body height multiplied by 4 for the perfect length. The butt of the pole should be as wide as the widest point on your palm before it gets pointed. The pole should be straight as an arrow, completely smooth from top to bottom, and have a pointed butt.

Step #7 - When all the poles are peeled and smoothed, it is time to point the tree butts or bottom of the poles. The pointed pole grips the Earth during setup and greatly stabilizes the Lodge for extreme weather. The point reduces pole surface contact with wet Earth, thus reducing the pole's "wicking effect" or moisture absorption from the ground up, ultimately extending the pole's life. Start by standing it vertically and resting it against a tree or something tall that can support it. Rest it at about a 45-degree angle and use the hatchet to chip away the bottom 8 inches of the pole into a point about half an inch in diameter at the very bottom. Then, rest the pole horizontally on your pole horse workstation and use the drawknife to continue shaving the whole point until it is smooth. Go all the way around but not trying to make the point sharp so it narrows to about half an inch in diameter and there are no rough spots that could tear the cover.

Step #8 - Take your freshly peeled, smoothed, and pointed poles ready to be dried either to an area where they can be set up as the lodge frame or hung on three ropes hanging from a tree or outside overhang so they lay horizontally suspended in the air. If you already know how to set up a proper lodge frame, then set up your tripod and put all the poles in place without wrapping the final rope. Just leave the poles loose. Over the course of two to three weeks, check your poles often and turn any poles that may have started to bow while drying. Turn the bow so it sticks out from the frame, and gravity will help straighten it out. If you stay on top of this process, you should have a beautiful set of straight, dry, and ready-to-be-pitched poles.

If there is wet weather when your poles are ready to be dried, you can take 3 half-inch ropes about 5 feet long each and hang them like dangling U-shapes about 8 feet apart on an outdoor porch or overhang with 2x4 or 4x4 wood beams, making sure the bottoms of each "U" are the same distance from the hanging point. Alternate your poles as you lay them into this hanging bundle by laying one tip first, then putting the next one butt first until all are in place. This allows gravity to evenly weigh all the poles down on each other, straightening every pole and allowing good air circulation as your poles dry. Wait about two to three weeks, checking every few days to see if they stay straight. If you see one bending, pull it out of the bundle and try to slide it back in lower in the stack with the bend pointing up so it can straighten out. Once the poles by either method are dry and ready, celebrate this ancient art of original architecture.

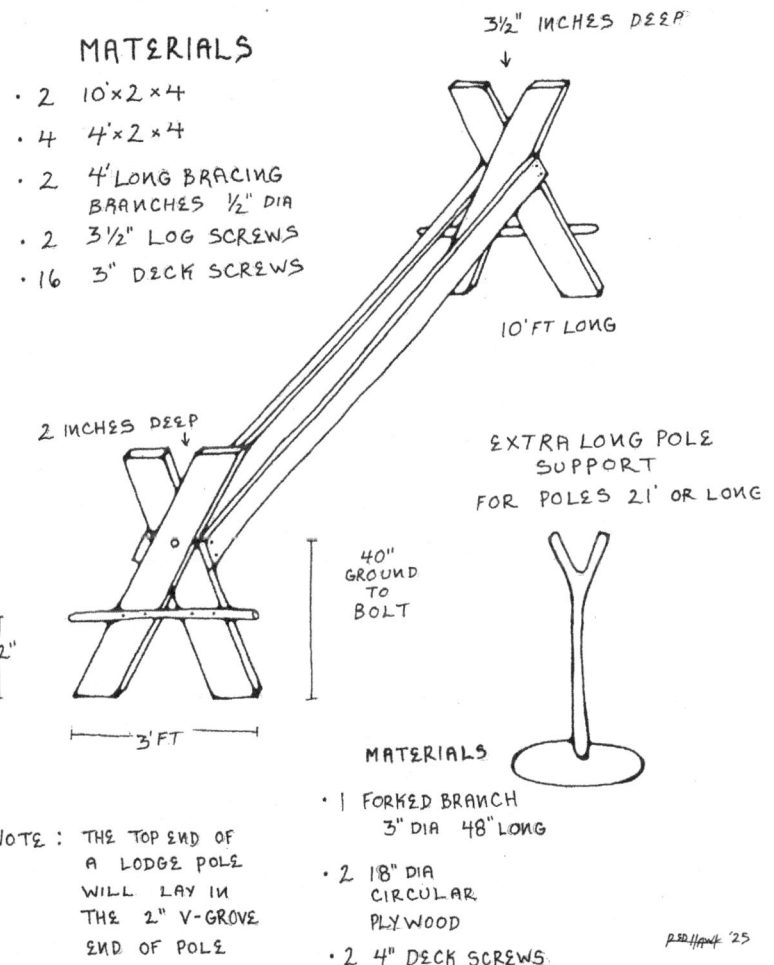

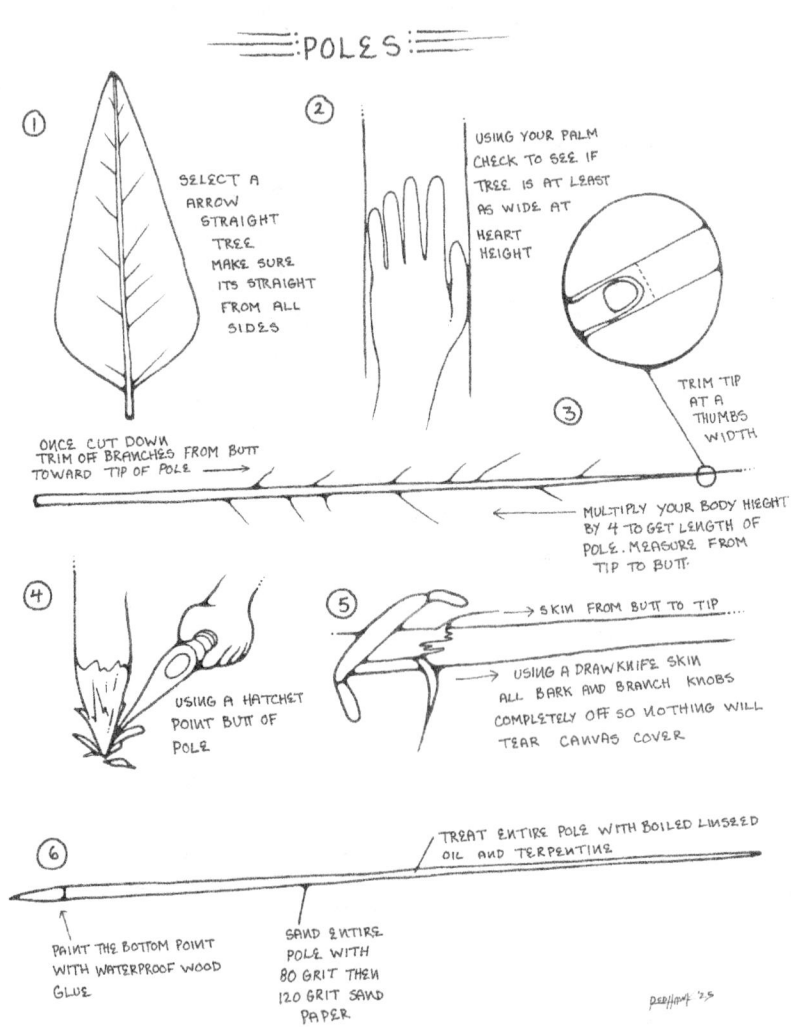

CHAPTER 12

SACRED MEASUREMENTS

To build the sacred home and temple for our physical body to exist in harmony and balance on Earth, we must design our spaces to fit our bodies like a custom pair of shoes. Grandmother Lodge is designed from Nine Sacred Measurements from our bodies that allow us to design a Lodge to hold our mind, body, spirit, and soul perfectly.

The Nine Sacred Measurements:
1) Full Body Height
2) Ground to Throat
3) Ground to Navel (belly button)
4) Elbow to Fingertips
5) Hand Length (wrist to fingertip)
6) Hand Width (widest part of your palm)
7) Two Fingers Width
8) Three Fingers Width
9) Foot Length

These Nine Sacred Measurements give us the 24 measurements necessary to design a Lodge Cover:

1) Full Body Height
- Body height multiplied by 3 gives the radius of the lodge cover
- Smoke flap length
2) Ground to Throat
- Height of doorway
3) Ground to Navel
- Length of the gores
- Distance multiplied by 2 gives lengths for large tie tapes

4) Elbow to Fingertip
   - Length of the bottom edge of smoke flaps
   - Length of small tie tapes
   - Distance divided by 2 gives a radius for large main canvas reinforcement
5) Hand Length
   - Length of the tie flap
   - Width of the tie flap
   - Distance between lacing pins
6) Hand Width
   - Width of the front left and right hems of the lodge cover
   - Width multiplied by 2 gives the diameter of small canvas reinforcements
   - Length of leather lacing pin reinforcements
   - Width of large tie tapes
7) Width of Two Fingers
   - Spacing between front right hem lacing pin holes
8) Width of Three Fingers
   - Space between front left hem lacing pin holes
   - Width of leather lacing pin reinforcements
   - Width of small tie tapes
9) Foot Length
   - Foot length multiplied by 3 gives us the distance for the pitch or drop from the cover's radius point down to the base of the tie flap
   - Distance measured downward from top corner edges of the cover to angle front edge of cover before hemming
   - Foot length multiplied by 3 gives us the distance between stake cords
   - Width of Gores
   - Width of leather smoke flap reinforcements

9 SACRED BODY MEASUREMENTS

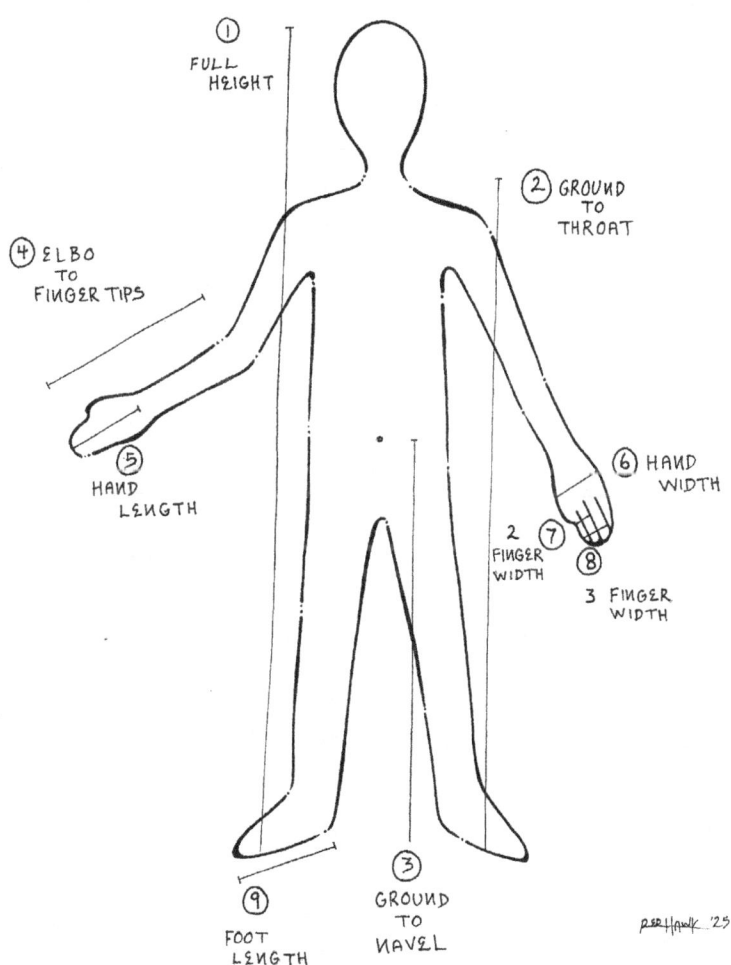

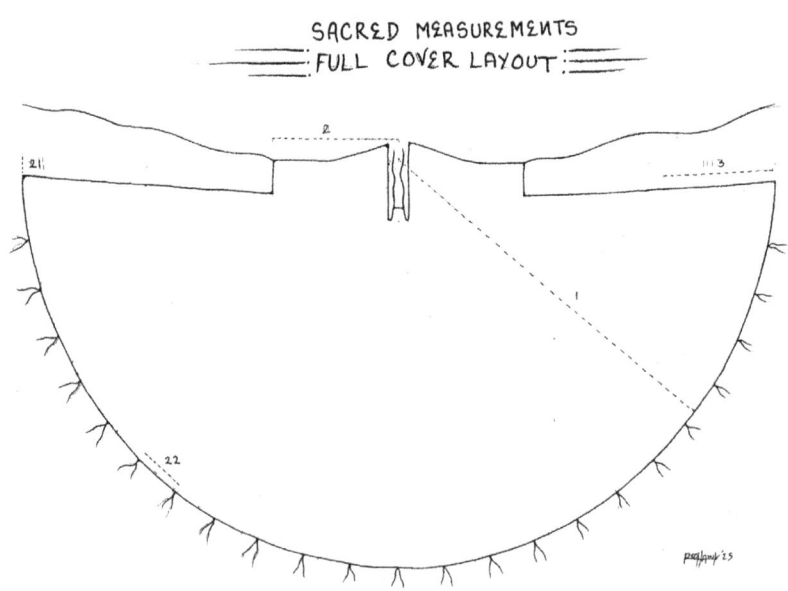

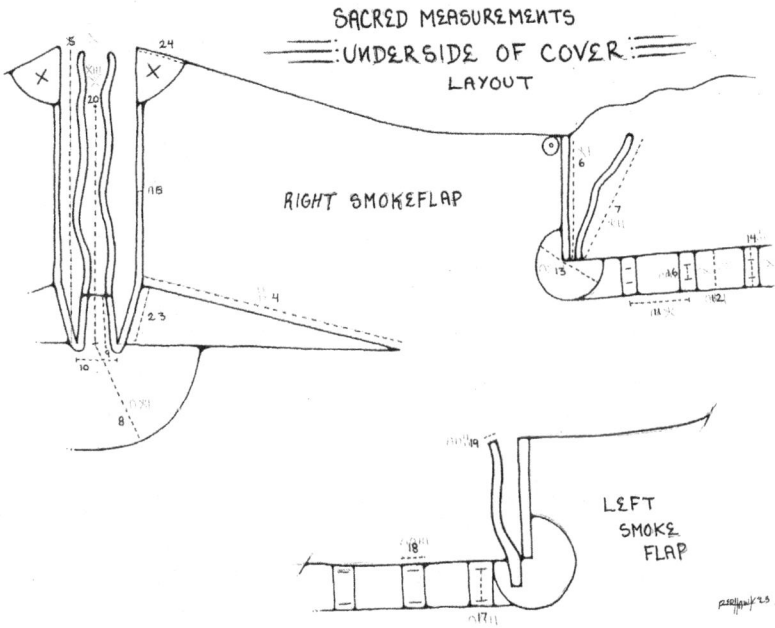

CHAPTER 13

COVER

Section 1 - Canvas Layout

Materials for Lodge Cover:
- Choose your canvas yardage in 63-inch wide 100% unbleached natural cotton 10 to 12 ounces army duck canvas. See steps 1- 6 to find the number of yards you'll need.
- Two spools of #90 poly UV-resistant thread (1,000 yards each)
- 2 to 3 square feet of 8mm or thicker buffalo or cow leather
- 100 feet of 7/16 inch thick 100% cotton cord
- (27) ¾ inch diameter round river stones completely smooth - to find how many you need for your cover, do this equation: Body Height multiplied by 3, multiplied by 2, multiplied by 3.14, divided by 2, then divided by your foot length in inches multiplied by 3, then divided by 12. This will give you your stone count for your peg loops.

Tools needed to make the Cover:
- Industrial sewing machine with size 16 or 18 needles
- Fabric scissors
- ¾ Chisel
- Small hammer
- 24 feet of thin rope ¼ inch or less in diameter
- Thin round metal tent stake about 12 inches long by 1/8 inch thick

- Superglue (2 tubes)
- Fabric pins
- 4-foot T-Square
- Leather hole punch 1/8 inch in diameter
- Measuring tape

Step #1 - Before anything else, get your measuring tape. Hold the end of the tape in one hand and stretch your arms straight out to your sides to get an accurate length of your arm span. The average adult will be about five feet in length. Make sure you stretch your arms until you feel a pull on your shoulder muscles. This pull is the feeling you use to stop stretching your arms when using them to measure out the rope, canvas, and other Lodge materials using only your body. Make sure you get as accurate a measurement with the tape as possible. You will use this method to measure out your canvas from the roll.

Step #2 - With the tape measure, find your body height. Multiply your body height by 3 to get your cover radius. So, if your height is 5 feet 6 inches tall, your lodge radius will be 16 feet 6 inches. On paper, write down radius = (your measurement). Now multiply your radius by 2 to find the length of the longest piece of canvas for your cover. If your radius is 16½ feet, you should get 33 feet, then add 2 feet to this so your first piece will be 35 feet long. The equation for canvas strip #1 = radius multiplied by 2 plus 2.

Step #3 - Take the final length of canvas strip #1 and subtract 1 foot from it to get the length of canvas strip #2 for your cover. The equation for canvas strip #2 = Length of strip #1 minus 1.

Step #4 - Take the length of canvas strip #2 and subtract 4 feet from that to get the length of canvas strip #3. The equation for canvas strip #3 = Length of strip #2 minus 4.

Step #5 - If you are above 5 feet tall, you'll need a 4th canvas strip. The equation for canvas strip #4 = Length of strip #3 minus 7.

Step #6 - If you are 6 feet 6 inches or taller, your cover will require five strips of canvas. The equation for canvas strip #5 = Length of strip #4 minus 14.

Here is a chart showing the body heights to canvas specifics so you can get an idea of what you'll need for your cover:

Body Height Ft	Radius Ft	Canvas Strips	Strips in Ft	Yards
4	12	3	26, 25, 21	24
4.5	13.5	3	29, 28, 24	27
5	15	3	32, 31, 27	30
5.5	16.5	4	35, 34, 30, 23	41
6	18.0	4	38, 37, 33, 26	45
6.5	19.5	4	41, 40, 36, 29	49
7	21.0	5	44, 43, 39, 32, 18	59

Section 2 - Measuring Out Canvas Strips with Arm Spans

Lay the bulk canvas roll on a clean, smooth floor at your feet, with the length of the roll spanning left to right from your perspective while you stand at the center point of the role with your feet flat on the floor. Make sure you can see the cut end of the fabric on the roll to easily bend down and pull up the canvas to unroll what you need. Most adult people will have an average height of five feet from the floor to the height of their hands while they extend out their arms. So, we count by fives while unrolling the canvas by hand. This method is helpful for making covers when working in little spaces.

To start:

- Bend down and pull up the end of the fabric roll to about head height.

- Repeat, counting by 5 until you unroll what you need for your cover strip.

- When you've unrolled the estimated amount you need, go back to the cut end or beginning of the unrolled fabric. Starting at the corner of the factory edge of the loose canvas, with one hand pinch the very corner and stretch out your arms, pulling the canvas tight between hands to measure out an arm's distance of fabric.

- Pinch tight and bring the fingers on the very corner to the point of your other fingers on the canvas without moving from your measurement point.

Do this until you've measured out your desired amount accurately. When you've reached the last arm spread for measurement, have your scissors available to make a cut of about ¼-inch on the edge of the canvas where your fingers were holding the final measurement.

This method takes patience and detailed attention and will work every time you measure out the canvas. Now cut a clean straight line from the ¼ inch cut to make sure you cut the end of your strip squared off, ensuring the next strip starts out clean.

As you measure each strip for your cover, make sure you mark or sort each strip to know which one is which, for the smoothest sewing. I like to only cut out the next strip I'll need to sew when making covers, so I don't have the "opportunity" to grab the wrong one and waste two hours of sewing a seem 40 feet long, which you'll have to undo.

Section 3 - Sewing Canvas Strips

All Amarukhan Lodge covers are sewn with strips of 5 feet 3 inch wide canvas laid out horizontally, layered with the longest strip on top and each under strip being consecutively shorter. All seems are non-fold flat seems that are shingled with the top layer overlapping the one underneath, which creates a most efficient rain runoff. Having the least amount of canvas layers allows any part of the cover to dry out as fast as possible, reducing or preventing mold and mildew from forming.

Step #1 - Get your first and largest canvas strip #1. Find one of the cut ends of the canvas and measure 6 inches in from the corner down along the full-length factory edge. Make a small mark with a pen or pencil on the edge. This is where you start to sew your second canvas strip to make the first seam. Sitting at your sewing machine, bring your first strip, bunch it up to the left of the machine, and feed just the factory edge with the mark 6 inches from the cut edge under the needle, ready to be lined to strip #2. Now bunch up canvas strip #2 and bring it to the machine leaving the big bundle on the floor to your right while bringing the cut end of the strip to strip #1 and making sure you start sewing with strip #2 under strip #1 and make a ¾ inch flat seam starting on your 6-inch mark. Run this seam twice through, making a ½ inch gap between the stitches. Your first stitch should be about 1/8 inch from the factory edge of strip#1. Then, stitch 2 is made ½ inch to the left of stitch #1.

Step #2 - At the bottom of strip #2 along the factory edge on the right corner (opposite corner to where you started sewing the first seam), measure 2 feet or 24 inches along the factory edge in from the corner. This will be the starting point for seam #2 as you add your third canvas strip. Now repeat the flat seam left overlapping right sewing technique as you did for your first seam. Two rows of stitching, 1/8 inch from the factory edge of Strip #2 as it overlaps Strip #3, and the second row of stitches is ½ inch to the left of your first stitch. If you are 5 feet tall or shorter, this will be your last seam to sew, and you'll be ready to cut out your cover. People 5 feet 3 inches to 6 feet 8 inches tall will have one more seam to sew. People 6 feet 9 inches or taller will have two more seams to sew.

Step #3 - If you are between 5 feet 3 inches to 6 feet 8 inches tall, your cover will have 3 full canvas strips, and the fourth strip will be generally narrower than the complete 5 feet 3 inches of the canvas width. At the bottom right corner of strip #3, measure 3 feet 6 inches from the corner along the factory edge to mark the sewing point for your fourth strip and third seam. Sew like you did all the other seams. Make sure your strips are shingled longer over shorter from top to bottom of the cover.

Step #4 - If you happen to be 6 feet 9 inches tall or taller, this is your next step. At the bottom right corner of the factory edge on strip #4, measure 7 feet along the factory edge to mark the sewing point for the fifth and shortest canvas strip on the cover. Sew it like you did the first seam. Make sure that strip #4 overlaps #5. This is a reasonably quick seam to sew. Once done, celebrate because the biggest part of sewing is done!

Section 4 - Canvas Cutout

Step #1 - Locate a big flat, preferably grassy, space at least 40 by 30 feet in size. Lay out your sewn cover completely flat with the outside of the cover (The side that has the overlapping seams going downward from the largest canvas panel to the smallest). Imagine water flowing from the largest canvas strip down toward the seams. Would it flow, or would the seams catch it?

Step #2 - With the cover laid out completely flat with no wrinkles, get your metal tent stake, 24 feet of small rope, pen or pencil, scissors, and a small hammer. Locate the very center point of the factory edge of the top of the cover along the longest canvas strip (this is the radius point) with the small metal stake, pin it through the canvas at this center point about ¼ inch from the very edge of the canvas. This is point (A). The stake holds this point of canvas to the Earth and gives us the mark where we will later design the cover from this point.

Step #3 - Tie the very end of your small rope to the stake; the rope makes a good cord for drawing out our half-circle lodge pattern. Pull this rope straight across the canvas to the center point on the bottom canvas strip, and make sure the rope is taught.

Step #4 - Now tie your pen or pencil onto the rope, so when the rope is tight, the pen/pencil is straight up and down, and the point falls short, no more than an inch from the bottom edge of the cover. Where you tie the pen is the radius distance you'll draw the cover out with. Now test the centeredness of your radius point by swinging the radius rope from one top corner of the laid-out canvas as though you were drawing out your cover. Check to see if the pen/pencil goes off the edge of the canvas at "any" point. If it does, tie it shorter on the rope or adjust your radius point stake so the pen/pencil swings as close to the canvas edges and corners as possible without ever falling off the edges, and that so the pen/pencil swings evenly around the cover, not too close to one edge and far away from the edge on the other side.

Step #5 - The goal is to maximize our canvas use and reduce our scrap material. When you are confident your canvas is flat, your radius point stake is perfectly centered, and your pen rope is measured to the proper length, go ahead and slowly draw out the half circle on your cover.

Step #6 - Leave the canvas flat and cut out the cover, starting on the top right corner of the flat "outside up" canvas, going clockwise until reaching the left top edge of the cover. Once cut out, first fold up and remove the scraps with your beautiful half-moon cover flat on the Earth.

Section 5 - Design Layout

We're ready to map out our cover with the canvas sewn together and cut out, and our Nine Sacred Body Measurements are written down. After the cutout, leave the cover flat on the Earth to draw out the cover detail lines before bringing it inside.

Step #1 - Pitch

In your Nine Sacred Measurements, get your foot length in inches. Multiply this number by 3. This is the length of the pitch of a real traditional Lodge. The Lodge is not a perfect cone but rather a cone slightly tilted back. This pitch does several things to the outcome of a Lodge:

> • The pitch creates an oval or egg-shaped floor shape instead of the perfect circle that would come if the Lodge were a straight cone. This oval gives more structural stability during high winds.
>
> • The pitch of a Lodge creates a longer area in the front of the structure from the point of the apex of the poles to the front of the Lodge, and a shorter length in the very back of the structure from the apex of the poles to the back of the Lodge. This tilt in the cone gives a Lodge much more wind resistance when the front of the Lodge

faces the opposite direction of prevailing winds, which push against the more vertical backside of the Lodge and forces the poles in the front of the frame to push into the Earth.

• The pitch creates the tilt of the cone, which also creates more headspace in the back of the Lodge when inside. The back is the honorable living quarters in a Lodge.

• The pitch also shifts the place of the smoke hole on a Lodge from being in the very top center of the cone to moving it forward to the longer front side, which means your fireplace is about 1½ feet closer to the doorway, also adding living space in the back of the Lodge as well. When it's raining on a Lodge, the central rope holding the frame together saturates with water and will drip, so having the fireplace moved forward avoids this small drip and allows it to fall on the Earth altar behind the fireplace.

Step #2 - Tie Flap

Get your pitch length (foot length in inches multiplied by 3.) Let's say you get 30-inches. Go to point (A), where the stake made a tiny hole on the cover's top edge when you drew your circumference line. That central radius point is the point from which the whole Lodge design is focused around. At the radius point on the top of the cover, measure your pitch distance straight down from point (A) and make a dot. This is point (B). Now, get your hand length measurement; let's say it is 7 inches. Divide that in half, you get 3.5 inches. Measure 3.5 inches directly out from the left and right of point (B), the central dot you just made. These 2 dots are points (C). So, what you see is 3 dots in a row, left to right, the width of your hand length. This is the base of the tie flap on the cover. From points (C), take your T-square, lay it on the cover from the radius point (A) to each point (C), and draw a line connecting each dot (C) to the radius point (A). You should see a long pyramid shape with the 2 lines a hand width apart at the bottom and meeting on the radius point at the edge of the canvas. This long cone shape will become your tie flap.

Step #3 - Gores

From your Nine Sacred Measurements, get the ground-to-navel distance in inches. This will be the length of the gores or smoke flap extenders. At the bottom of each line you just drew for your pitch, points (C) measure going toward the left from the left point and toward the right from the right point, so your yardstick is parallel with the top edge of the cover. Draw the two lines the length of your navel to ground measurement. From the end of these lines measure going back towards the starting point of the line your hand length and make a mark on the line. These are the gore lines, your ground to navel distance minus your hand length. Those lines are where we attach the gores later. From the (C) points, measure 2 inches out on the gore lines and make a mark. This gives a little space between the tie flap and where the gores get sewn onto the gore line.

Step #4 – Front Edge of Smoke flaps

From your Nine Sacred Measurements, get your complete body height. Go to the radius point (A) on the cover and measure from that point out along the top factory edge in both directions your body height and put one mark on either side of point (A). These 2 points (D), mark the front edge, total length, and bottom corner of the smoke flaps.

Step #5 – Bottom Edge of Smoke flaps

From your Nine Sacred Measurements, get your elbow-to-fingertip measurement. Go to the point (D) marks you just made with your body height, and from the points (D) on the edge of the canvas, go perpendicular from the edge line, measure down, and draw the line of your elbow to fingertip length. These are the lines for the bottom edge of the smoke flaps. The bottom of these lines are opposite of points (D), they are points (E).

Step #6 - Front Hems

Take your foot length, go to the top corners of the cover, and measure down the cut edges on both sides. Mark this distance down both side edges of the cover; these are points (F). Get your hand width measurement and measure starting from points (F) upward toward the top edge of the cover. Add your thumb width to this hand width measurement for the full hem width, and mark both sides of the cover, these are points (G) and should be between points (F) and the corners of the cover. Each corner of the cover will have two marks (F) and (G). The first point (F) will determine the final circumference of the cover. Points (G) are the width for the second canvas layer in the front hem of the cover.

With a pencil, draw a straight line using your yardstick from point (F) to the bottom of your lines from step #5, points (E). These are your hemlines from the bottom of the smoke flaps to the bottom edge of the cover.

Using your hand width measurement, measure from point (E) up the line that is the bottom edge of the smoke flaps, and make a mark, point (H). Mark both sides of the cover. Using your yardstick, draw a pencil line from points (H) to points (G). These lines mark the full width of the front hems and the canvas that gets folded under to create the second layer of the front hems.

Step #7 - Stake locations

The final step in mapping out our cover is marking where the stones and cotton cord peg loops will go around the entire perimeter of the bottom edge of the cover. With the cover laid out completely flat, fold it in half so it becomes a quarter circle. Make sure the cover is lined up with all edges as perfectly as possible, and the whole cover is as flat as possible. Locate the very bottom center point of the cover, which is at the bottom of the fold on the very edge of the canvas. This is the bottom center of the cover. Mark the inside of the fold point (I). Get your foot length in inches and multiply it by 3 with the cover still folded. Say you got 30 inches. After multiplying your foot length, start at point (I), the bottom center crease, measure out, and mark every 30 inches going along the cut, curved edge of the cover, marking both layers of canvas until you reach the top corners of the cover. If your last measurement brings you 12 inches or less to point (F) on the edges, skip making this mark. However, if it's more than 12 inches away from point (F), make this final mark on both edges of the cover. You have finished laying out your stake points and finished the design of your new cover.

Section 6 - Lock Stitches

Step #1 - This is a seemingly small physical step in Lodge making, but I assure you it is important. OK. Now we have our strips sewn together, the cover cutout, and we have seams with unfinished ends. Depending on the size of your cover, you might have 4 open seam ends or up to 8 if your Lodge is over 20 feet in diameter. These seam ends must be finished with a stitch to prevent the seam from unraveling. I like to use a smaller stitch than I did on the seam, but not too small because the canvas is thick. I start at the edge of the canvas on the seam and begin about 1/8 inch in from the edge, sewing a rectangle 2 inches long and as wide as the overlap of the seam about ½ inch wide.

Step #2 - Once the rectangle is sewn, stitch a second row over one side of the rectangle, then stitch a zigzag pattern inside the rectangle from one end to the other. Use super glue and run it along the very edge of the canvas on the seam to add a final touch.

You may ask why I am not hemming the edge of the cover. My answer is old-time Canvas Lodges were seldom hemmed because it's a lot of sewing, and when you use stone and cord peg loops, there is no tension on the bottom edge of the cover once pitched. Also, a hem on the bottom adds layers of canvas, adding an area along the entire bottom of your Lodge that will now take longer to dry out in wet weather. Either way, the bottom edge is always the first to mold on a cover, so take extra awareness around this when you have your Lodge set up. A cotton lodge cover can mold in three days if untreated.

Section 7 - Front Hems

Step #1 - Using your scissors, cut from point (D) to point (H). Then cut from point (H) to point (G) to remove this canvas strip from the corner of the cover. Do this to one side of the cover only. I finish one hem completely before starting the other one, so we don't have weak points from cutting that could tear while we move canvas around to sew. Call this strip the tie tape strip and put it aside.

Step #2 - Cut from point (H) to point (E). Remember we added our thumb width to our palm width when we measured out from point (F) to point (G). On the edge of the canvas between points (H) and (G), fold your thumb's width under the cover to make a clean edge for our front hem. Iron it well. Now fold the line from points (E) to (F) under the cover and iron well. You should have a clean edge double layer hem the width of your palm running from the bottom edge of the smoke flaps to the edge of the cover.

Step #3 - On the sewing machine, run a stitch on both edges of this hem along the whole length. At the bottom of this hem, which is the edge of the cover, do a lock stitch a 1/8 inch from the edge of the fabric and about 2 inches wide across the whole width of the hem. Put superglue along the bottom canvas edge of the hem to prevent any excess fraying on the heavy wear point at the bottom of your Lodge, getting daily wear and tear from going in and out.

Step #4 - Now repeat steps 1 through 3 for the other half of the cover.

Step #5 - Get a scrap from what you cut off the cover when you cut out the circumference of the cover. Cut 2 strips that are three fingers wide by 18 inches long. Fold them in half and iron them smooth. Unfold them and fold each edge lengthwise about halfway to the center crease. Iron both folded edges smooth. Fold each strip again on the center crease and iron it again. These are four-layer, finished edge tie tapes that will be sewn later at the tops of each front hem used to tie the front of the cover together around the frame poles. Run a row of stitches along each edge on both tie tapes. Finish with a lock stitch on one end of each tie tape. Put tapes aside.

Step #6 - Get another piece of scrap canvas and draw two circles in diameter as wide as both your palms put together. Draw circles at least two inches away from each other. Then make a dot in the very center of each circle. With a straight edge, draw two lines from these center points on each circle at 90-degree angles so each circle looks like a perfect ¼ slice of pie has been removed. Now cut out each circle, so it has the slice removed. When you cut, make sure to cut ¾ of an inch out from the lines, so you have an extra perimeter of canvas to fold and hem on the final reinforcements.

After you've cut out both ¾ circles, cut out triangle sections along the ¾ inch extra canvas around the perimeter every 1 inch to create tabs that you fold under and iron. Do this to both pieces, so they have their edges folded clean to the original line we drew when making the circle. Take each piece and trace it on more scrap canvas. Cut out these ¾ circle traces to 1/8 inch inside the trace line so that these second pieces will fit under the tabs of the first pieces, creating a beautiful 2-layer, hemmed edge, reinforcements that go on the top of the front hems of the cover and the bottom corner of each smoke flap, where Lodges receive a lot of tension at these points.

Step #7 - Get 2 scraps of canvas and cut two rectangles 3 fingers wide and an inch or two longer than your elbow-to-fingertip measurement. Fold this strip in half and iron well. Then unfold it and fold both edges again halfway to the center crease. Iron both folded edges. Now fold the middle crease and iron again to end up with a 4-layer edging piece that goes along the bottom edge of the smoke flaps.

Step #8 - On the bottom edge of the smoke flaps in the corner where the front hems meet the smoke flaps, we're going to sew our ¾ circle double-layer canvas reinforcements to the underside of the cover (the same side you folded the hem.) Place the circle so the 90-degree angle lines up perfectly with the top of the hem and the bottom of the smoke flap. Place reinforcements, so the tabs are on the underside when placed on the cover. Make sure you're on the inside or underside of the cover, so the reinforcements cover the top raw edge of the hems. Now stitch 1/8 inch in from the edge of the reinforcement around its perimeter. Do 2 more rows of stitch about ¼ inch in from the first one, just sewn around the perimeter. Once you have 3 rows of stitches around the perimeter, do a zigzag stitch inside the innermost row of stitches to lock the reinforcements in place. Sew zigzags from top to bottom of the inside stitch and across the whole reinforcement.

Step #9 - Get the first strips of edging you made in step #5. These will be tie tapes sewn right beneath the bottom of the smoke flaps where you just sewed the reinforcements. However, the left hem overlaps the right front hem when setting up the Lodge. So, you have to sew one tie tape on the underside of the front left hem and sew the other tie tape on the outside of the right hem, so when the cover comes together, the tie tapes are hidden between the 2 edges of the Lodge cover. Sew each tie tape below the bottom of the smoke flap on the area where you sewed the reinforcement. Start sewing 2 inches in from the edge of the hem so the tie tapes line up in the middle of the hem when tied together. Sew them on with lock stitches.

Step #10 - Get your second pair of strips you made to be used as edging, each one should be just bigger than your elbow to fingertip measurement. Open the folds and place the bottom of each smoke flap with the raw edge into the fold. Make sure the edging is tight up against the corner with the ¾ circle reinforcement, and this edging should go over the reinforcement along the bottom edge of the smoke flap. Double check to make sure the smoke flap is as far into the edging as possible. Now run two rows of stitches down the edging to secure it on. Do a lock stitch on the inside end of the edging near front hem. Then, cut the other end of the edging clean with the edge of the smoke flap. Run your superglue along the trimmed edge. And as soon as it's dry, do a lock stitch on the same end to finish the edging. Do this to both smoke flaps.

Section 8 - Gores

Step #1- Get the ground to navel and foot length measurements from your Nine Sacred Measurements. Get a big scrap of canvas and draw 2 separate lines with the yardstick the length of your ground-to-navel. On one end of each line, measure your foot length up from one end of each line and make a dot. Use the yardstick and draw the second lines connecting the other end of the first lines to the dots, making a long "V".

Step #2 - You should have long "V"s, with each line being ground to navel length. The open end of the "V" should have the ends of each line be your foot length apart. Now connect the open ends with a pencil line to complete the triangle. You should have 2 triangles drawn out on scraps, separated from each other.

Step #3 - Get your scissors and cut these gores out ½ inch outside of the perimeter of each triangle to have material to fold in and clean up the gore edges. But, cut out the short side of the gores exactly on the lines. Once cut, you should have 2 long triangles with a ½ inch hem along the long sides and no ½ inch hem along the foot length side of the gore. Get your iron and fold both long edges on each gore ½ inch under and iron them smooth. Your gores are cut out and hemmed.

Step #4 - Starting at the radius point on the cover, point (A), cut down one side of the tie tape to point (C). Cut from point (C) along the "gore line" we made in Part 5, Step #3 of the design layout, to the mark set a hand length from the end of the gore line. Cut out one gore line to this mark. Fold the canvas on each side of the cut gore line ½ inch over or on top of the cover, creating a ½ inch hem. To hem this area, we're going to attach the separate gore. Iron the hems on the cover well. Make sure to remark the point 2 inches out from point (C) on the gore line again. Do this on the bottom line, making sure there's space between the gore and the tie flap.

Step #5 - You have 1 gore line opened up and hemmed, ready to have the first gore laid on and stitched. Bring a gore to the gore line with your 2-inch mark. Make sure the hem on the gore is folded under the gore and ironed well. Line the bottom corner of the wide end of the gore to the 2-inch mark. This gives more room for sewing and edging later. Starting on the mark, sew along the edge of the hem on the gore, making sure the hem of the gore is right on top of the hem on the gore line. Stitch straight to the small tip of the gore. Make sure the end of the gore line cut on the cover lines up to the middle of the gore underneath it when you reach the point sewing the hem where the gore continues to get sewn onto the cover past the cut line. This gives a good amount of attachment space for sewing. Bring the top corner of the gore to the hem on the smoke flaps side of the gore line. Measure 2 inches in from the end of the smoke flap hem so the gore stays in alignment with the opposite side. Bring the unstitched corner of the wide end of the gore to this new 2-inch mark on the top side of the gore line and stitch along the hem edge straight down until you reach the endpoint of the gore and your first stitch line.

Step #6—Now go back to the bottom corner of the gore where you started sewing and stitch a second row ¼ inch inside the top and bottom rows of stitching on the hems.

Step #7 - We cut the gore line on the cover a hand length shorter than the actual gore so we could have enough room to lock stitch the end of the gore onto the cover. Go ahead and lock stitch the gore from the end of the gore line cut or split in the cover fabric to the end of the gore, which should continue on top of the cover for a hand length for extra attachment space. Don't worry about the raw cut edge on the shortest side of the gore. We put trim on that later.

Section 9 - Center Tie Flap Reinforcement

Step #1- Get a big scrap of canvas, and with a pencil, draw a line that's your elbow-to-fingertip length. Divide this length in half and use that number as the radius length to make your initial line into a half-circle. Mark the center of the elbow to the fingertip line to make your radius point; from that point, you can draw out the half-circle. Once that is made, use your hand length, say it is 7 inches, divide that by 2, which is 3.5 inches, and use that measurement to mark 3.5 inches in both directions on either side of the radius point along the top flat edge of the half circle. This is the width for the base of the tie flap on the reinforcement. Draw straight lines up a hand's length from your 2 marks on either side of the radius point and square it off so it's a rectangular extension centered at the top of the half-circle. Now cut out ¾ inches outside the perimeter line of the whole reinforcement shape so we have material to hem and fold under. Cut out little triangles every inch around the ¾-inch hem material only along the curve of the reinforcement. Leave the hem around the rectangle on the top of the reinforcement as is. Fold and iron all tabs and hemlines around the reinforcement.

Step #2—On the Cover, you should have a tie flap with a base the length of your hand and a long triangular tie flap extending out between the smoke flaps. Fold this strip two times down onto itself, creating a three-layered narrowing tie flap as long as your hand. Iron the tie flap well.

Step #3 - Get your cutout half-circle reinforcement, so the top edge of the reinforcement is right on top of the bottom hemline across the gores. The rectangular extension on the reinforcement should line up on top of the tie flap in the center of the cover. Trace the shape of the tie flap on the reinforcement, trim the reinforcement leaving ¾ inch of extra material around the tie tape trace lines to hem the reinforcement.

The entire perimeter of the reinforcement will have ¾ inch tabs to fold and hem when cut out. This holds the second canvas layer underneath and creates a beautiful, hemmed edge on the reinforcements. Go ahead and cut it out, fold it, and iron it well!

Step #4 - Trace your reinforcement on scrap canvas. Cut the trace out 1/8-inch inside the perimeter line so the shape will fit under the tabs of the first layer. Fit the second layer of canvas under the hem tabs on the first layer and iron the whole reinforcement. Your main reinforcement is now ready to sew.

Step #5 - Make sure your cover has the "inside" facing up for this step. The reinforcement goes on the underside (inside) of the Lodge cover. When you're sure the inside is facing up, bring the completed 2-layer reinforcement to the top center of the cover, so the top edge of the ½ circle sits right on top of the bottom seams on the gores. The reinforcement should turn your 3 layered tie flap into a finished 5-layer tab. Start by stitching across the top edge of the half-circle and sewing around the perimeter of the half-circle only. Don't sew the tie flap yet! Do 3 rows of stitches around the half-circle perimeter. Then do a giant zigzag lock stitch across the whole half-circle. Now sew the tie flap layers together using one continuous spiral stitch starting along the bottom edge of the tie flap clockwise until you stop in the middle.

Section 10 - Smoke Flap Edging and Tie Tapes

Step #1 - In Section 7, step #1, we set aside 2 long strips cut from the cover when we were creating the front hems of the cover. Cut out 2 strips a hand-width wide, and your ground to navel measurement multiplied by 2 for length.

Fold and iron these strips in half lengthwise. Then unfold them, fold the edges halfway to the center crease, and iron both sides, 3 folds in all. Fold the main crease again to make two edging pieces about 7 feet long and 4 layers thick for the smoke flaps.

Step #2—To attach these edging strips to the smoke flaps, start at the top edge of a smoke flap and open the edging so it can fully cover the material. Extend the strip about an inch past the corner of the smoke flap so there's extra material to cut clean with the flap edge angle.

Start sewing from the top corner and place your first stitch in the middle of the strip. Sew about six inches at a time as you put the edging down the smoke flap. Then continue the edging around the curve from the smoke flap over to the tie flap in the top middle of the cover. This is tricky to sew, so hold the edging tight and do your best. Continue sewing up the tie tape till the end. You should have about 3 feet left of edging that goes past the tie flap. This extra edging will tie the cover to the lift pole. Sew 3 rows of stitches lengthwise down the entire length of edging tapes.

Step #3—Place the cover on a flat surface where you can extend the top edges of the smoke flaps and trim the excess edging from the corners. Finish both ends of each smoke flap edging with four lock stitches, using lock stitches at each end.

Section 11 - Lacing Pin Layout

In this section, we're going to bring the front hems of the lodge cover together, lining them up starting at the bottom of the smoke flaps to mark both hems simultaneously as we lay out our lacing pin guide marks. This ensures a perfect lineup with both front edges of the cover for proper Lodge setup.

Step #1 - Fold the cover in half so the front hems are lying flat against each other and lined up evenly, starting with the base of the smoke flaps. With the cover laid flat on the ground, smooth out the entire length of the hems as they lay one directly on top of the other. Use your fabric pins, and starting at the bottom of the smoke flaps, pin both layers together, making sure the very edges of the hems are perfectly lined up. Put a pin about every foot so the entire hem stays together while we make our lacing pin marks.

Step #2—Get your ground-to-throat measurement. Go to the bottom edge of the pinned hems and measure up the hems. Mark the very edges of both layers of canvas. This is where the top of your doorway will start.

Step #3 - When you pinned together the hems with the bottom of the smoke flaps lined up and worked your way to the bottom edge of the hems, you will see either the very bottom edges lined up perfectly or the more common one is a little longer than the other. This is due to how we drew out the radius curve. If one is longer, trim it with scissors so both hems are the exact same length.

Step #4 - Starting at the mark you made for the top of the doorway, use your hand length and measure going up the hems making marks on the fabric edges a hand length apart from each other. Continue until you reach the bottom of the ¾ circle reinforcement at the top of the hems. You should have an average of 8 to 12 marks depending on cover size.

Step #5 - Go to the hems' bottom edge, measure 2 inches up, and make a mark on the canvas edges. This is where the very bottom lacing pin will go. Now measure 1 hand length up from that mark and mark off the second bottom lacing pin position. I put 2 lacing pins at the bottom of my doorways. Your lacing pin locations are now laid out. Go ahead and pull out all of the pins.

Step #6 - Taking both hems into consideration, count all your lacing pin marks - generally between 16 and 24 marks. Using the widest part of your palm measurement, cut out as many leather lacing pin reinforcement pieces you need. They should be rectangles as wide as your palm and 3 fingers thick.

Step #7 - If your cover is laid out flat and has the outside facing up, stand at the top part of the cover where you'll be facing the smoke flaps. Here you'll have the front hems of the cover to your left and right. Remember, the left hem overlaps the right when facing the cover from this direction in Lodge setup, so make sure you know which ones are the top and the bottom layers. Left is the top, and right is the bottom. With your leather reinforcements, you'll sew them on the "outside" of the cover on the left hem and the underside of the cover on the right hem. When the cover is pitched, you'll see the leather on the outside of the lodge and on the inside.

To sew on the reinforcement, lay 1 across the hem and make sure the mark on the canvas edge lines up with the top edge of the reinforcement. Stitch a 1/8-inch stitch inside the edge around the perimeter of each piece of leather. When they are all stitched onto a hem, run a stitch down the exact middle of the hem until you reach the bottom edge of the cover. Done right, you should have run that central stitch down the middle of each leather reinforcement. Do this to both hems.

Step #8 - On the left front hem with the leather sewn on the outside, measure from the middle of each leather reinforcement 3 fingers width, by placing your middle finger over the center stitch on each reinforcement and holding your pointer, middle, and ring fingers together flat on the leather. Make a dot on both sides of your fingers in the middle of the leather. You end up with 2 dots 3 finger widths apart marking the points where the slits for the lacing pins go. Do this to all the leather on the left hem.

Step #9 - On the right hem leather reinforcements, measure 2 fingers width from the center stitch evenly in both directions. You'll have 2 dots 2 finger widths apart on the leather reinforcements of the right hem. These are smaller because the right hem goes underneath the left hem when pinning the lacing pins, so the holes are closer together to allow each lacing pin to slide through easily.

Step #10 - Get your ¾ inch chisel and a small hammer. Put a piece of flat wood board underneath the reinforcement that you're going to make punch slits for the lacing pins. Put the chisel vertically on each dot, marking the lacing pin holes. Line the chisel exactly center or evenly between the top and bottom edges of the leather before you hammer your slit. Punch all holes for the leather reinforcements. Keep the chisel blade parallel to the edge of the hem when you make your slits to ensure the lacing pins will slide through effortlessly.

Section 12 - Smoke Flap Leather Reinforcements

Step #1 - Cut out a square of leather that is your foot length on each side. Cut from one corner to another across the square to make 2 matching triangles.

Step #2 - Cut out 2 circles of leather that are as wide as your wrist in diameter.

Step #3 - On the top corners of the smoke flaps, you will sew your triangular leather reinforcements. Make "sure you sew them on the outside of the cover." They will be slightly bigger than the angle of the corners you are sewing them to, so don't worry; make a mark on the leather along the edge of the canvas to trim the leather to the exact angle of the smoke flap corner. Once trimmed, stitch 3 rows ¼-inch apart from one another around the perimeter of the leather. I like to stitch a 2½-inch square in the center of the reinforcement to provide extra security to the area where we will run the smoke flap pole through.

Step #4—Sew your 2 leather circles to the bottom outside corners of the smoke flaps. I run just 1 stitch around the perimeter of the leather circle, about 1/8-inch from the edge.

Step #5 - Get your ¾ inch chisel and hammer with your board under the leather corner reinforcement and punch a 2-inch "X" in the center of the triangle.

Step #6 - Get your 1/8-inch hole punch and punch a hole in the center of each circular leather reinforcement at the bottom of the smoke flaps. This is where we run our smoke flap cords from.

Step #7 - Cut two pieces of cotton cord, each 15 feet long, and tie a knot at one end of each cord. Then, run the cord through the holes punched in the leather, ensuring the knot rests against the leather. Finally, burn the ends of each cord to prevent unraveling.

Section 13 - Stone and Cotton Cord Stake Ties

In Part 5, Step #7, we mapped out the points (I) along the bottom edge of the cover where our stone and cotton cord stake ties will be placed. Let's put 'em on!

Step #1—Cut a piece of cotton cord 2 feet long for each mark along the bottom of the cover, generally 18 to 24. Burn the ends of the cords to prevent the ropes from unraveling.

Step #2 - Lay your lodge cover flat with the outside facing up.

Step #3 - Place a stone underneath the cover at your marks - about 4 inches up from the edge. Take a 2-foot cotton cord, and from the outside, where the canvas covers the stone, tie a half-square knot in the middle of the cord around the canvas and stone. Pull out the wrinkles as best you can around the stone. Then tighten the half knot and finish it off with a full square knot. You should have 2 strands about 9 inches long of cotton cord dangling from around the stone. When you tie them off, ensure that the knot is facing the bottom edge of the cover and that the cords point downward.

I use the stone and cotton cord method of making stake loops for a few reasons. #1 - You can move them if the ground is too hard in an area. #2 - Having the sacred stones as a part of your home is grounding and helps the Lodge move Earth energy.

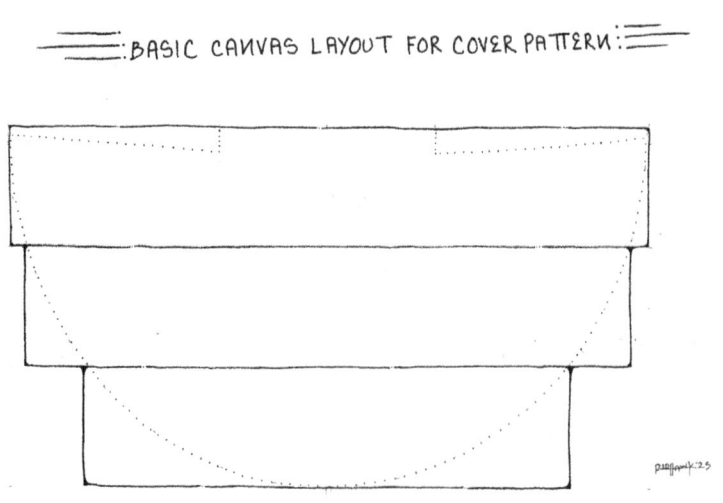

FINISHED COVER CANVAS LAYOUT PATTERN

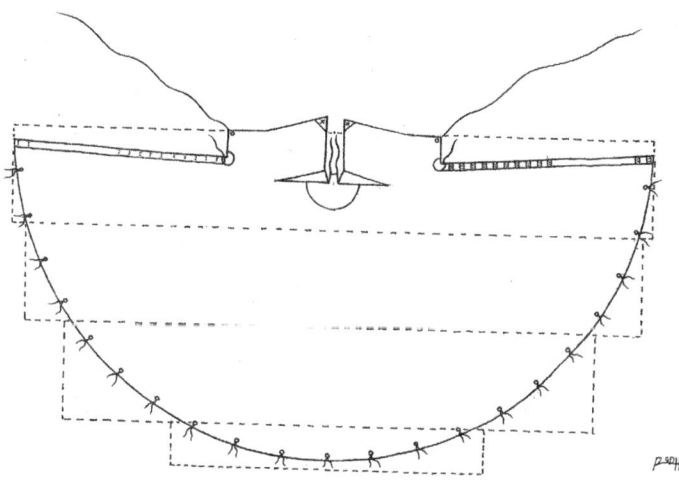

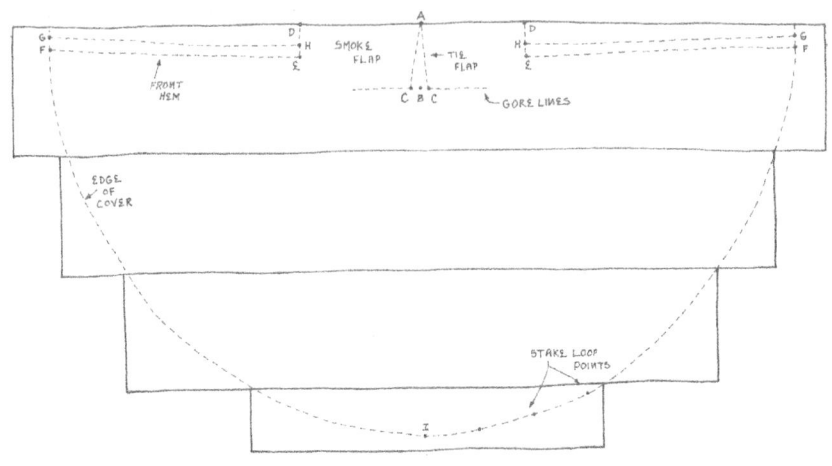

MAPPING OUT A COVER
WITH
SACRED MEASUREMENTS

STITCHES:
FOR BASIC COVER PATTERN

DOUBLE STITCHED
MAIN SEAMS

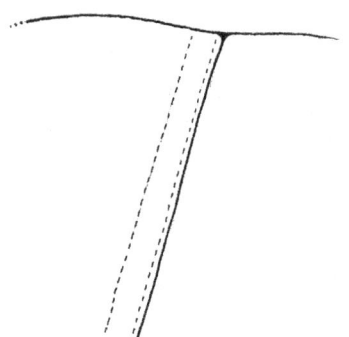

MAIN SEAM
RAW EDGE
LOCK STITCH

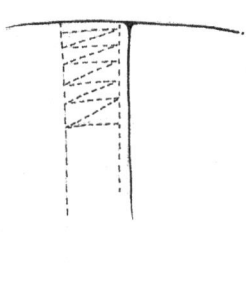

FRONT MAIN
HEM TRIPLE STITCH

FRONT MAIN HEM
TRIPLE END STITCH.

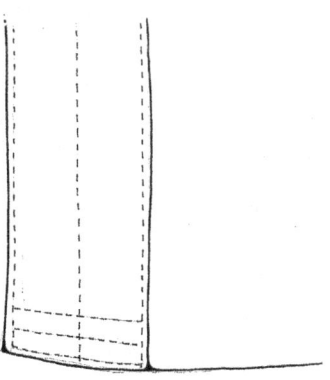

STITCHES
FOR CANVAS REINFORCEMENTS

SMALL

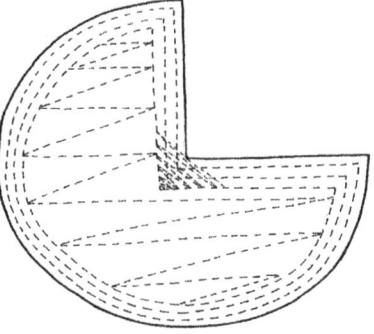

LARGE

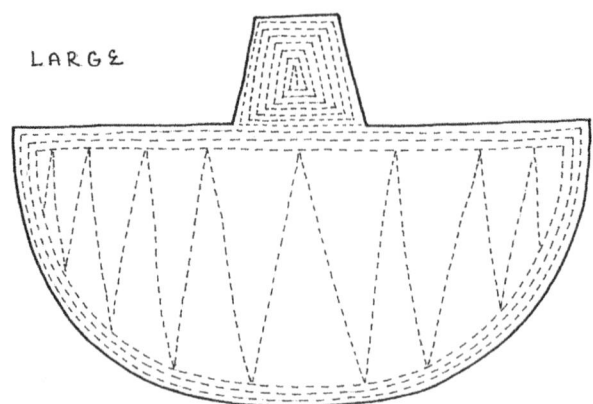

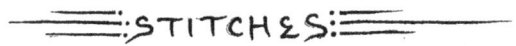

BOTTOM EDGE SMOKE FLAP EDGINGS AND TIE TAPES

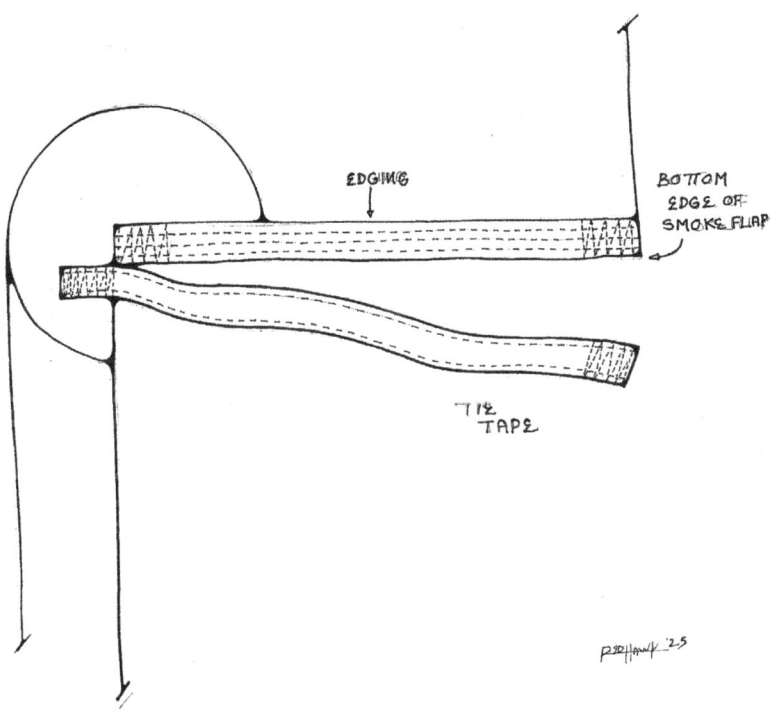

STITCHES

TOP EDGE SMOKEFLAP EDGING AND TIE TAPES

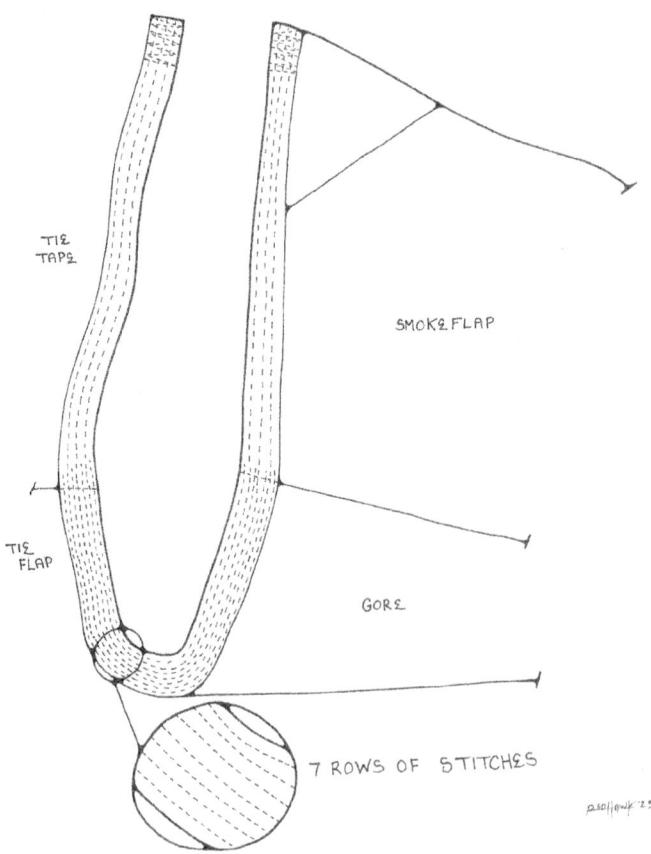

STITCHES
LEATHER REINFORCEMENTS

SMOKEFLAP
POLEHOLE REINFORCEMENT

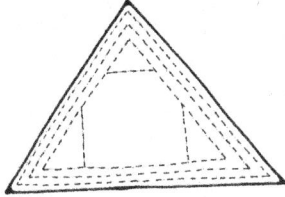

SMOKEFLAP CORD
REINFORCEMENT

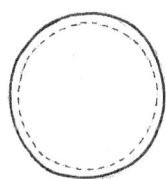

LACING PIN
REINFORCEMENT

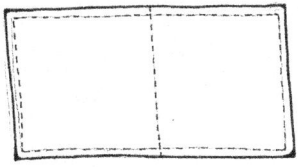

CANVAS REINFORCEMENT PATTERNS

BOTTOM EDGE SMOKE FLAP DOUBLE LAYER REINFORCEMENT

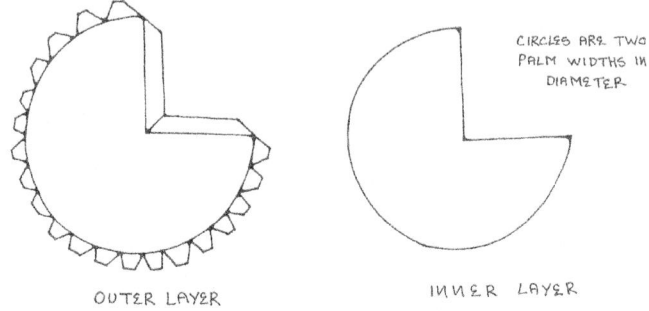

OUTER LAYER   INNER LAYER

CIRCLES ARE TWO PALM WIDTHS IN DIAMETER

LARGE CENTER DOUBLE LAYER REINFORCEMENT

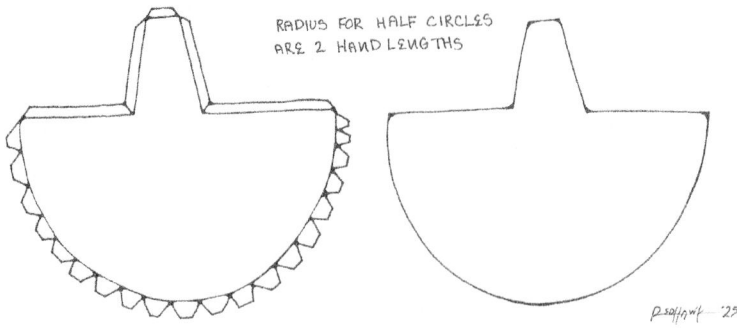

RADIUS FOR HALF CIRCLES ARE 2 HAND LENGTHS

COVER HEM AND EDGING
PATTERNS AND FOLD LINES

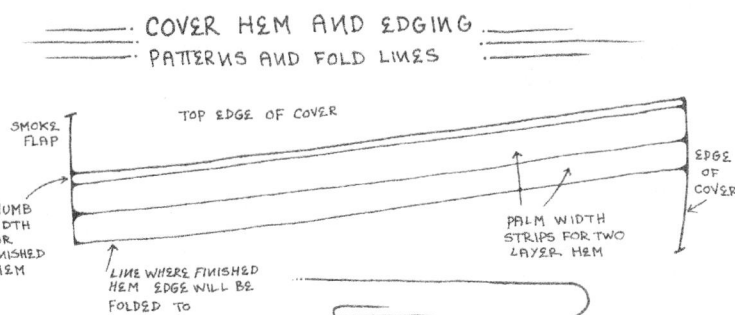

GORE PATTERNS AND FOLD LINES

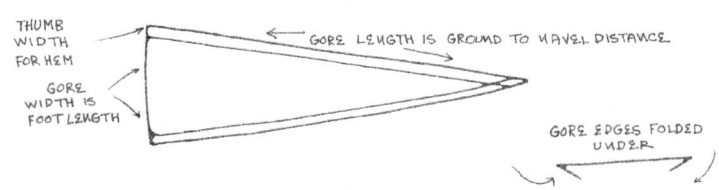

EDGING AND TIE TAPE PATTERN AND FOLD LINES

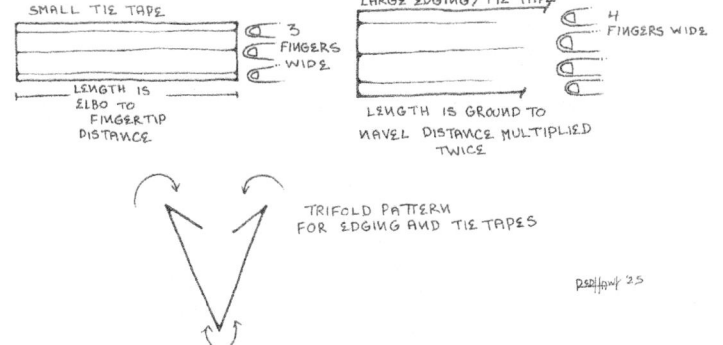

GORES

1 MARK 2 INCHES IN ON GORE LINE

MARK HAND LENGTH IN FROM END OF GORE LINE

CUT ½ INCH PAST GORE LINE FOR HEM

2 HEM OPENED GORE LINE AND REMARK 2 INCHES FROM END

CUT AND HEM TO MARK ON LINE

3 SET GORES WIDE END CORNERS ON 2 INCH MARKS TO START SEWING

4 TRIM SMOKE FLAP EDGE CLEAN WITH GORE

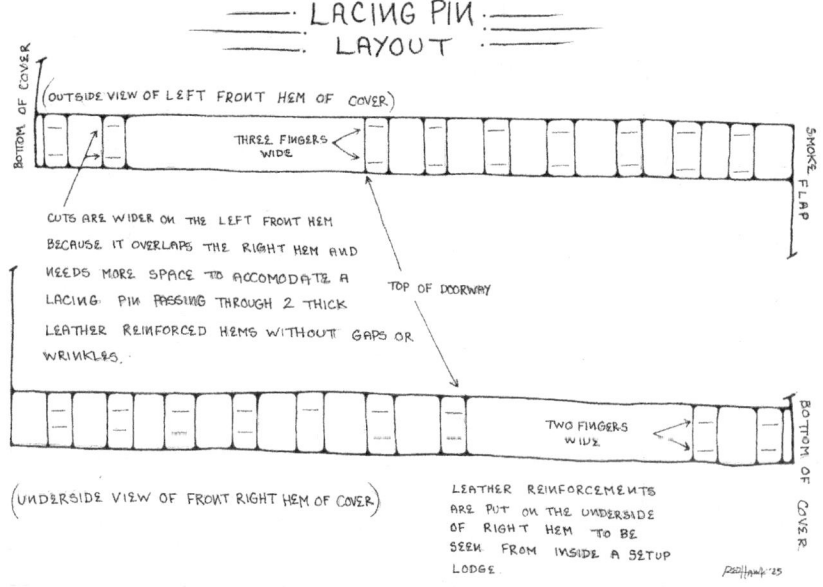

TYING THE STONE COTTON CORD PEG LOOP

① PLACE A SMOOTH ROUND STONE AT BASE OF FINGERS IN PALM

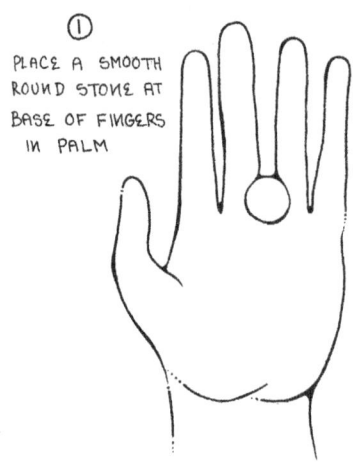

② PINCH CANVAS EVENLY AROUND STONE.

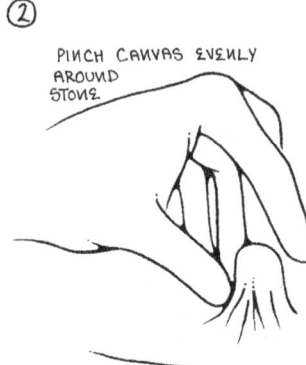

PUT HAND WITH STONE UNDER EDGE OF COVER TILL COVER EDGE MEETS FIRST WRINKLE IN WRIST

③ TIE A COTTON CORD AROUND CANVAS AND STONE SO KNOT IS ON BOTTOM OF STONE

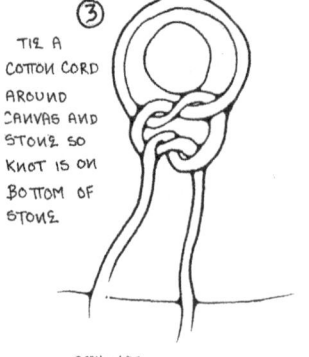

④ TRY TO PULL OUT WRINKLES IN CANVAS AROUND STONE WHILE TIGHTENING KNOT

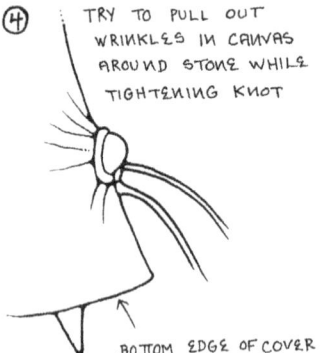

BOTTOM EDGE OF COVER

CHAPTER 14

DEW CLOTH

Materials:
To find out how much canvas you'll need for your dew cloth, follow these 2 equations:

(cover radius in feet multiplied by 2, multiplied by 3.14, divided by 2 = cover circumference) and (cover circumference in feet plus 6 extra feet for overlapping, divided by 3 = yards of canvas needed)

- 54 feet of 7/16 inch cotton cord, cut into (27) 2-foot lengths
- Superglue (several tubes)
- 50 feet of ¼ inch sisal rope
- All of the scraps left from making your cover should be cut into 1-foot-wide strips as long as each scrap piece will allow. Cut as many as needed to have enough strips to cover the circumference of your lodge cover plus 10 feet.
- (30 or 38) 3-inch long, 3/8-inch diameter branches used under the rope as rain channel sticks

Tools:
- Scissors
- 1/8-inch leather hole punch
- Sewing machine
- Size 16 or 18 needles
- Branch pruners
- #90 UV resistant thread

Section 1 - Panel Design

No matter what size Lodge it is, making a dew cloth remains the same. Using 5 foot 3-inch-wide canvas, I make a 3 section dew cloth comprised of 4 panels per section with 2 extra feet on every section for overlap. To complete the design, each section has a scrap canvas ground contact strip sewn along the entire bottom edge of each dew cloth section. To start, we have to design individual panels that will fit the circular shape of the Lodge.

Step #1 - Get your lodge circumference in feet. Add 6 feet for overlap to this measurement. Divide the total by 12, then divide that answer by 12 again. This gives the length in inches for the bottom edge of a panel.

Step #2 - To find the length of the top edge of the Dew Cloth panel, do this equation:

(Lodge radius in feet, minus the width of the dew cloth canvas which is 5 feet 3 inches or 5.25 feet. Multiply that answer by 2. Multiply that answer by 3.14. Divide that answer by 2. Add 6 to that. Divide that answer by 12. Divide that answer by 12 again = Length of the top edge of the panel in inches)

It helps to draw this out for future reference. See the illustration and make one like it. These equations give you the measurements for 12 panels total, using 4 panels per section, for a beautiful 3-section Dew Cloth.

Step #3 - Find an area where you can unroll your dew cloth canvas for at least 20 feet. Start to pattern out your panels so the first one is right side up, and the next one is upside down, and so on. This maximizes canvas usage.

Section 2 - Sewing

Step #1 - Cut out your 12 panels and get your iron hot so you can hem the edges of your panels. I like to have a shingle effect with the dew cloth seams. Overlapping from left to right with four panels making a section, lay 4 on the ground and mark the outermost edges to be double folded into finished hems. Then, fold the left-sided hems once on top of the canvas and the right-sided hems once under the canvas. This pattern will allow you to be able to lay the left panel over the right, overlapping the ½ inch hems and stitch a nice 4-layer seam. "But that's just what I like to do." Please make whatever kind of seams you like.

Step #2 - I sew 2 rows of stitches down each seam and finish each row of stitches with a lock stitch at the bottom of the dew cloth.

Step #3 – Once a 4-panel section is sewn together, fold the entire top edge of the dew cloth over to create a 2-layer hem about 1½ inches wide. Stich a row 1/8 inch to each inside edge of the hem leaving the middle of the hem free of stitches. Make this fold toward the backside of the dew cloth.

Step #4—Get your 1/8-inch hole punch and punch a hole between the stitches of the top hem right next to each seam and one hole in the top hem at the center point of each individual panel. Each dew cloth section will have nine holes. Put superglue around the outside perimeter of each hole to prevent canvas tears.

Step #5 - Get all scraps from your cover and cut them into 1-foot-wide strips as long as the scraps allow. Make sure to square off all ends to each strip. Sew these strips together to make 3 long strips, each as long as the bottom edge of a dew cloth section.

Step #6 - Sew each scrap strip to the bottom edge of each dew cloth section with a single stitch. This makes it easy to replace later if it rots, molds, etc.

Step #7 - Cut 27 cotton cords 2 feet long each and burn the ends to prevent fraying. Slide them into the hole at the top of each dew cloth section. Don't tie them. They should stay in place. Your dew cloth is finished.

Step #8 - Get pruners and cut 30 sticks for a 17 pole lodge or 38 for a 21 pole lodge. They should be small sticks, straight, the width of your smallest finger, and as long as your palm. These are used as rain channels under the rope when hanging the dew cloth.

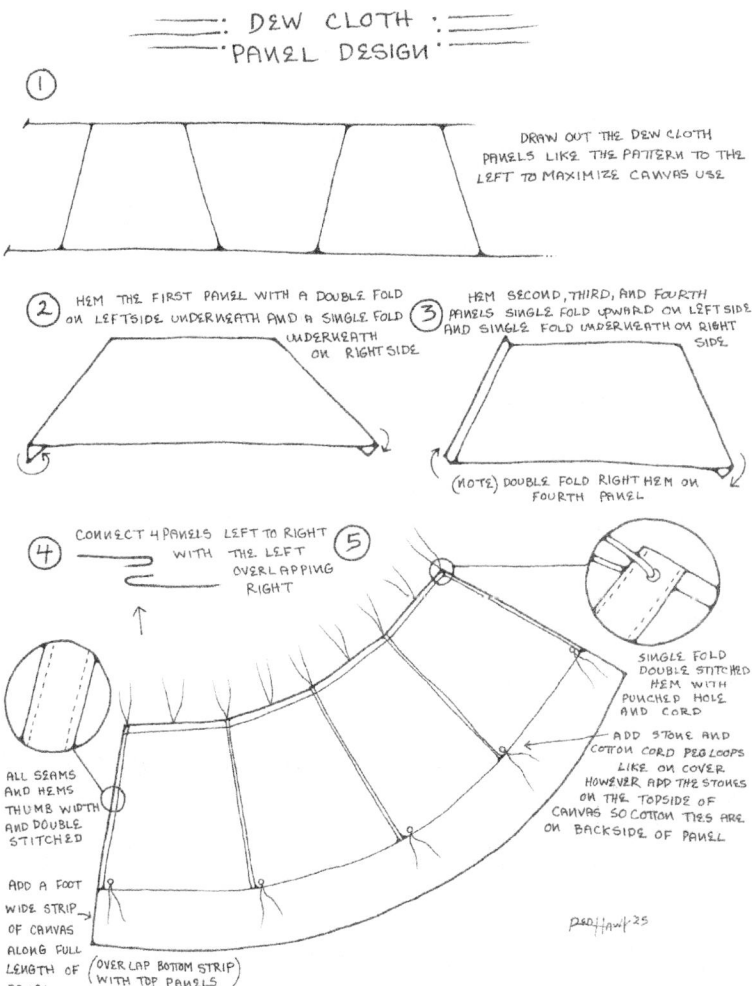

CHAPTER 15

DOOR COVER

Materials:
- One arm span of 63-inch full width canvas (about 5½ feet)
- (3) 2-foot-long leather cords about ¼ inch wide
- One piece of leather 6x6 inches

Tools:
- Sewing machine
- UV resistant #90 poly thread
- Size 16 or 18 needles
- Scissors
- 1/8-inch hole punch

Step #1- Take your canvas and lay it out flat. Fold it in half, so the factory edges are on the top and bottom. Iron this crease well. It's up to you how you want your door shaped. I like to taper the top end where the hanging cord goes. This is the point to decide your door's shape. Make your cuts and adjustments.

Step #2—At this point, I'm going to hem all edges ½ inches folded to the inside so they're hidden when the 2 layers come together. Iron well!

Step #3 - Your doors are ready to be sewn together. Up 4 inches from the bottom edge of the door, draw 2 horizontal lines 3 inches apart from each other to create a channel for a branch to slide in and become an inner brace. Draw out another channel about 7 inches from the top edge of the door. I like 2 support sticks holding the shape of the door. Now stitch these lines making sure to leave the hemmed edge of the door open to put the sticks in.

Step #4 - Finish stitching 2 rows around the door's entire perimeter but be careful to avoid stitching the stick channels.

Step #5 - Get your piece of leather and cut out two 2-inch circles and two rectangles 1.5 by 2 inches.

Step #6 - Sew the leather circles in the top corners of the door cover and sew the rectangles onto the bottom corners of the door.

Step #7 - Punch holes in the center of all 4 leather pieces. Tie the 2-foot leather string at the top to make a handle to hang your door. Put a knot at one end of each of the other two leather strings and slide them through the holes in the leather circles. These are the ties to hold your door down in strong weather.

Step #8 - Find 2 straight branches about 2 fingers wide, cut them to length, and put them in the pockets on your door. You are done!

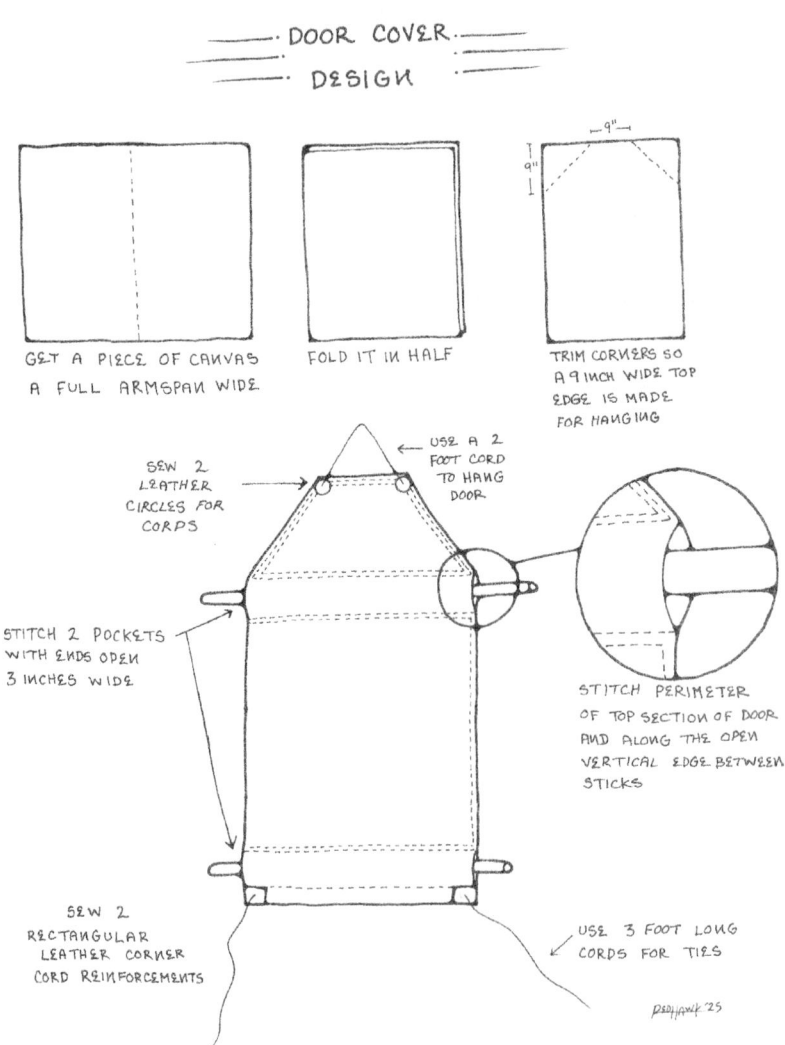

CHAPTER 16

STAKES AND LACING PINS

Part 1 - Stakes

I'm from Southern California, Ventureno, Chumash Country. In the hills there, you can find several hard kinds of wood; however, only a couple grow straight enough to make a good lodge stake. No matter where you happen to be, select a straight hardwood that's 1 to 1½ inches in diameter. I prefer Toyon for stakes as they are one of the harder woods and provide food as well. When pruning a fresh-cut stake, leave a branch stub on one end of the stake to prevent the cords from slipping off.

Step #1 - Once you've selected your wood type, cut your stakes to the length of your elbow-to-fingertip measurement. Make sure you cut a few extra and put the bundle aside somewhere out of the sun to dry for a couple of weeks.

Step #2 - Once dried, clean the stakes if needed to get rid of branch stubs, thick bark, etc.

Step #3 - Use your hatchet to make about a 2½ inch long point on one end of each stake.

Step #4 - Use your chisel to bevel the top ends of every stake to prevent splitting when driving them in.

Part 2 - Lacing Pins

You can find Willow growing along streams almost anywhere in the western United States. This makes my favorite lacing pins. They are arrow-straight, easy to peel, and always good medicine. What makes a good lacing pin is hardwood, as straight as possible and ½ inch in diameter. And last...the artistic touch you give it.

Step #1 - Cut the number of sticks you need for lacing pins plus a few extra. Cut them a little shorter than your elbow-to-fingertip measurement.

Step #2 - Measure off a palm's width on one end of each lacing pin. Mark it and score it with a knife to peel the bark off, leaving a palm width of bark as a handle grip on the largest end.

Step #3 - Using your knife, sharpen the other end of the lacing pin. It doesn't have to be sharp like a stake, but rather a rounded point that will help a pin push through the holes. Let them dry in a shady spot for a couple of weeks.

Step #4—If you feel inclined to paint your pins, please do. Lacing pin decorations is a long-time tradition. You are done!

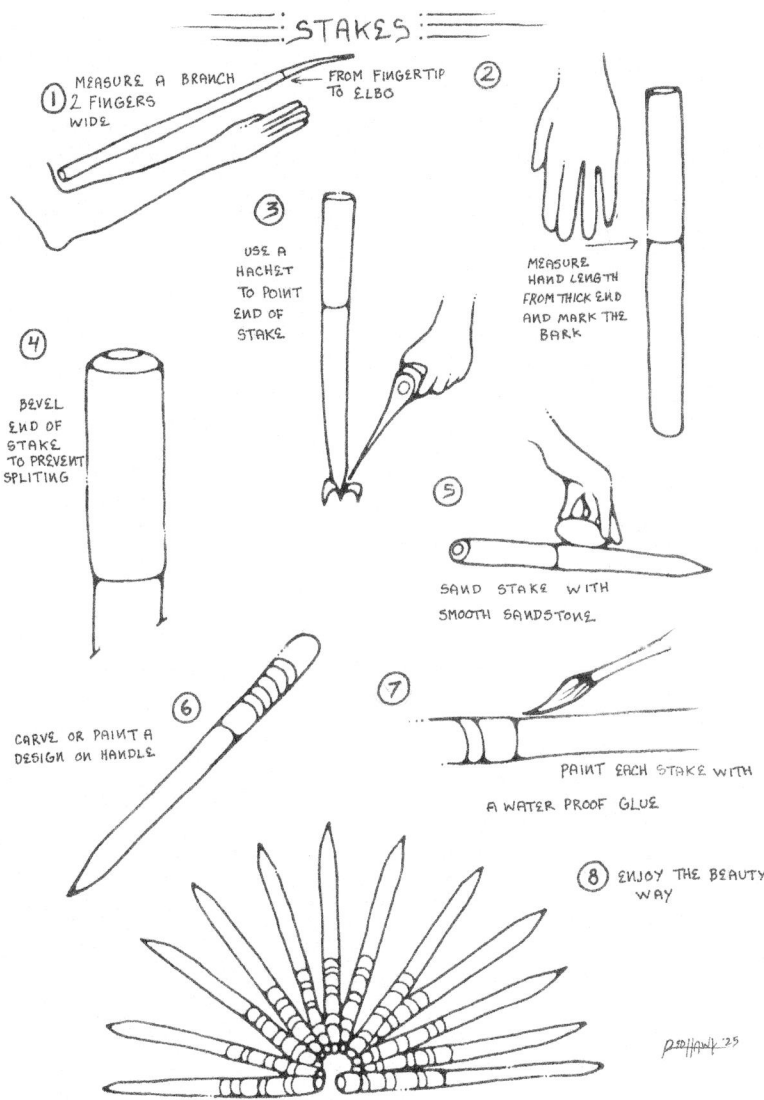

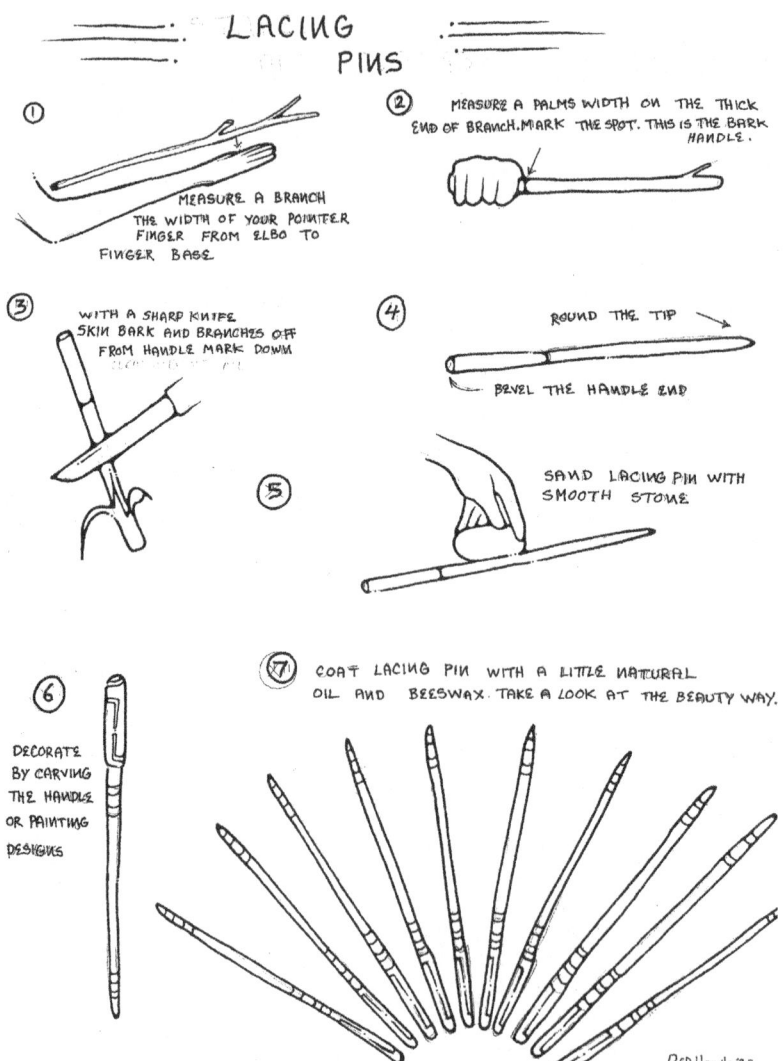

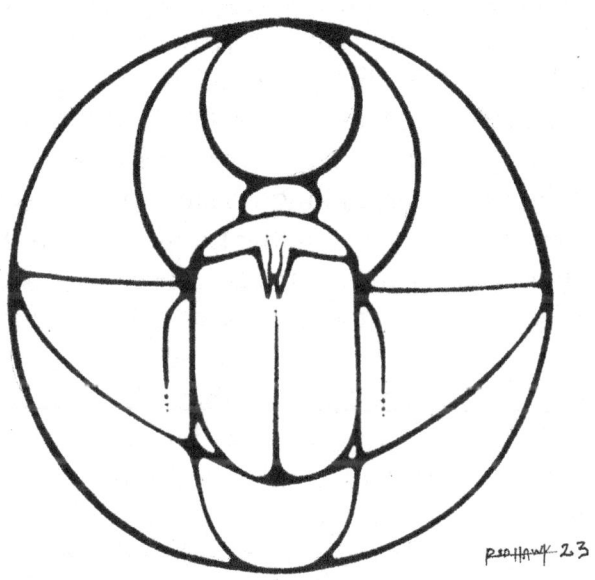

PART THREE: SET UP

CHAPTER 17

INTRODUCTION

Big up, this is a fun part of the book. I start by saying that this is a book written solely from my experience with Grandmother Lodge herself, knowledge I've been shown, or knowledge I have read. However, no matter what tradition someone has learned about the Sacred Lodge, one cannot compare another style of Lodge to an Amarukhan Lodge. Why? Because Spirit teaches everyone in the way that's best for their highest understanding. What I share is strictly from my personal experience in making Lodges. This is what works, appeals, and makes sense to me. So, please be open as I share my expertise in co-creating the style of the Amarukhan Lodge.

Our family is a migratory Amarukhan Band of the West Coast Red Bear Clan. Descendants of the Original Amarukhan People of Turtle Island. Originators of living pyramid culture, mound builders, and first growers of "American" cotton used in the first canvas lodges. The only documented Original People to be on Turtle Island soil 10,000 seasonal cycles before the "Native Americans" moved out to the Great Plains and adopted the Lodge lifestyle. We are not "Native Americans." We are the Original Amarukhans. Those who were on Turtle Island pre-Mongolian genetic dispersal and mixture. Ever wonder what happened to the real "Copper Colored Indians" the Spanish talked about in their journals from the 1400s? Just ask the Hopi Clans or the Modern Cherokee Nation today who the "Old Ones" were and who their influence was.

To pitch Grandmother Lodge is to enter a very ancient and sacred meditation. One aligns their thoughts to the elements, feels the Ancestors' guidance, and shows the Earth Mother that her children still have hearts and are putting their minds to good use. It is an honor to put up a Lodge, nothing less. The consciousness we enter while putting up a Lodge is a space that connects us with star knowledge and activates our highest potential. However, it takes years of practice and dedication fueled by the love of Grandmother Lodge to set one up silently at night with no moonlight. Practice again and again. Over and over. Focus on key setup steps and learn why you do something, not just how.

We have to understand we are working with powerful consciousness designed by the Creators, which works toward a different kind of perfection than the colonized way of thought. To learn to pitch Lodge is to learn to dance with the Earth, wind, fire, and water.

Lodge can be set up almost silently using little force and receiving little resistance. She is gentle. I have found that when you are trying too hard, stop! Something is off. There is a more fluid approach. Lodge teaches a lot. The more you understand why you do each setup step, the more you'll begin to feel the process with foresight and achieve the desired results. Be patient with yourself, knowing it's very important you learn to set up your Lodge entirely by yourself. This is very, very important! Practice, then practice more. Get to the point where you just love looking at the power of the pyramid. Study the techniques of setting up Lodge to understand the universal qualities. There is "no" right way, although some ways work more efficiently than others. Lodge will teach you what works for you.

To set up the Lodge properly, you need to know the Lodge's and your environment's nature. Everything is connected and relies on each other, just like setting up the Lodge. Every step has to be done right. You can't skip steps because each leads up to the next one. It is a simple, technical, natural, functional, spiritual, and self-building process.

CHAPTER 18

TRIPOD FRAME

Tools you will need:
- Shovel
- Pickaxe
- Rake
- 4-pound sledgehammer
- Small step ladder

Step #1 - Site Location

The lodge site location is crucial for a happy camp. Three things should be considered. We must first locate the site on the most elevated grounds available to ensure adequate drainage down and away from the Lodge. Second, the site itself should be pretty level, but it doesn't have to be perfect. A little variation in ground elevation is good. You want the frame to pitch in a balanced way. Third, the Lodge should not be pitched under trees. Pitch it out in the open to the north side of vegetation to receive shade, but avoid excess water, snow, branches, or whole trees that might fall throughout the year.

Use the shovel, pickaxe, and rake to level out the Earth, shaping an almost cosmic platform for Grandmother Lodge to land on. I prefer a level circular space 4 to 6 feet larger in diameter than the Lodge. I clear this space free of roots, stones, dry bushes, etc. You may leave small, unobstructive plants to decorate the Lodge. Make sure there's a soft-level space to put in your fireplace later. Use this time to ask the Earth permission to bring Lodge to the People. Consult with the animals and surrounding trees about your intent. Imagine you are preparing the Earth for your rebirth and thanking the ancestors for bringing you to Lodge. Seek their guidance to make sure your chosen location is acceptable. Take your time with this prep, for this is the foundation for the rest of your Lodge experience.

Depending on where you are, you may have a beautiful grassy field ready to go. You may also be in the desert, but wherever you are, there are times when one needs to put in floor covering to keep the dust down. I recommend putting a 3-inch layer of gravel or shale across the whole space. Some like to use sand, the choice is yours. The less you have to do to the Earth, the better. Remember that we must leave the campsite in better shape than when we got there!

Step #2 - Selecting Tripod Poles

No matter what size the Lodge is or the difference in pole numbers, we always follow the same procedure for tripod frame lodges:

- Select the 2 smallest poles in the bundle and put them aside to be the smoke flap poles.

- Choose the biggest pole in the bundle to be the lift pole or the pole to which we tie the cover.

- Out of the remaining bundle, choose the 3 largest poles to be the main tripod poles. The rest of the poles will fill in the frame in random order and need not be further selected for specific use.

Step #3 - Measuring the Tripod Poles the Old Way

Lay the lodge cover out with the leather facing up or the outside of the cover facing up and stretched out, ready to be measured. Follow with your eyes from the bottom corner of the smoke flap straight out to the edge of the cover. You will end up a little away from the cover as this is where the canvas was before hemming the front of the Lodge. Your heel should be in alignment with the bottom of the smoke flap. Walk heel to toe from the point at the top corner of the cover to the bottom center of the cover exactly halfway around the cover. Count your steps. The bottom center is the first measuring point we use. Mark it.

Let's say you took 21 footsteps. Divide 21 by 3. This would be 7 steps. Start again at the top corner of the cover and walk 7 steps along the edge of the cover toward the bottom center. Mark where your toes landed on the edge of the cover with your last step. This is the second point that we measure the tripod poles from and will be the spot where we lay the door pole to measure it for the frame.

Select the 3 poles we picked out for the tripod. These poles are the first poles we use to measure out the lodge frame. To measure the tripod poles, we first select the largest and smallest of the three poles, even if it's hardly noticeable. Each one is unique. Look for overall pole thickness and weight. Bring these 2 poles to the center of the laid-out cover. Lay them right on top of the cover, centered and together. They should lay from the bottom center stake loop to up between the smoke flaps on the top of the tie flap where the tie tapes extend off.

Use your hand on the butt of both these tripod poles to measure the full hand width of the pole sticking out past the bottom of the cover. This will create an air gap at the bottom of the cover once it is set up. Do this to both poles. Once the 2 poles are in place, run down the center of the cover over the tie flap down to a hand width past the bottom edge. Then, go over and look at the tie flap with the 2 small ends of the poles lying on top. Mark both poles where they cross the very bottom of the tie flap. This is where we tie the tripod together.

Bring the last tripod pole over and lay it on top of the 2 other poles. This is the door pole. The butt of the pole should land right on top of our previous mark on the cover when we walked one-third to the bottom center of the cover. Measure out a hand width for the pole butt to stick out past the edge of the cover, making sure the top end of the door pole lays across the other 2 tripod poles where we marked them near the top ends. Now mark the door pole where it crosses the poles, which all are directly over the tie flap. The door pole will be marked and measured higher than the other 2 tripod poles.

Now we will measure the distance from the bottom of the 2 center tripod poles in a straight line to the bottom of the door pole. Walk heel to toe in a straight line and count your steps. This is the measurement we use to space out our poles. We tie them together and call this the Ground Plan Measurement.

Step #4 - Tying the Tripod Poles
Select the 2 tripod poles that are marked together. Lay them out on the ground in your prepared space with the tips of the poles pointing toward the South. Make sure the bigger of the 2 poles is on the right side. Get the third tripod pole or door pole and lay the mark on it right on top of the marks of the other 2 poles. Lay the door pole from the apex out to the left of the other 2 poles. Measure out the ground plan distance from the butt of the 2 poles out toward the direction of East to find out exactly where the Butt of the Door Pole will rest (always facing East.) Once measured out, put a stake in the ground at the butts of the 2 poles and at the butt of your door pole.

Get the ½ inch frame rope and measure out 1½ arm spans (about 8 feet) of rope on one end. This is the length we need to tie the apex of the tripod. Stand inside the tripod as it lays on the ground so you're facing the South and the crown of the poles. Bring your rope where you measured 8 feet in and place that point of the rope on top of where the tripod poles all meet at the apex. Lay the 8 feet of the rope toward the left and let the rest of the rope lay to the right of the apex. First, we tie the poles with a full clove hitch knot. We wrap this knot from right to left around the poles. I use this saying to remember the clove hitch knot: over, under, over, and through. After the clove hitch is tied, wrap the rope above the clove hitch 4 times around the poles, keeping it slack-free but not as tight as you can pull. Finish the last 2 feet or so of rope by wrapping it around the top of the door pole above the main wraps. Tie it off with a half-hitch knot.

Step #5 - Lifting the Tripod

If your poles are over 20 feet long, it is helpful to place large stones at the butts to prevent sliding before attempting to lift them. Stand in front of the frame's apex, starting at where you tied the clove hitch knot. You should be facing North with the poles facing South on the ground. Lift the tripod at the apex with your focus going to the 2 poles together. Walk your hands down the 2 poles as you raise the frame.

Once the frame is nearly vertical, grab the biggest pole farthest to your left and start pulling it toward you in a southern direction until you feel the clove hitch tighten up and begin to make a creaking sound. The trick to knowing where to place the pole we swing out is threefold. First, it should be the same distance from the door pole as the other pole we didn't swing out. Second, when you look at the crown on the poles after swinging the pole out, you should see a "V" from the door pole and the North tripod pole. The pole you swing out should have its tip visually right in the center of the "V," creating a balanced "W." Third, the North pole and the South pole we swing out are several feet closer together than the distance from the rear poles to the door pole. Check these 3 things several times until you feel confident that everything is measured correctly. The extra rope hanging down should be hanging over the pole we swing out and kept in that position until all other poles are laid in.

Step #6 - Filling in the frame

Set up, in its final position, the tripod will be left alone and not going to move for any adjustments. Except when the cover goes on it may show a small adjustment needed in the frame. Looking at the tripod from the Eastern side, the door pole is always on the right side of the frame apex. A balanced "V" in the tops of the poles is the space into which we will lay all the other frame poles to complete the frame. The tripod makes 3 spaces to fill in with poles: a South Space, a North Space, and a West Space. If you cut 17 poles for your Lodge, you're going to lay 4 poles in each space. If you cut 21 poles for your Lodge, you're going to put 5 poles in the North and South Spaces and 6 in the West Space.

Start by placing the largest pole from the undesignated bundle of poles just to the left of the door pole with the pole's tip resting in the "V" at the top of the frame. Space it roughly 3 feet from the butt of the door pole. This makes the doorway on the Lodge and is the front of the Lodge. Lay another 3 poles into the South Space, four if you have a 19-pole frame. Each pole should sit right on top of the last one resting in the "V" going left from the door pole and all about 3 feet apart. Now start filling the North Space with the same number of poles you laid in the South Space, again, 1 at a time, but this time laying them going to the right of the door pole going right, with the top ends all resting on top of each other inside the front "V" of the crown. Space all these 3 feet apart.

It's time to fill in the West Space or back of the Lodge frame. Stand to the back of the frame, so you're facing East. Look up at the crown, and you will see a small "V" opening in the center of the pole tops. This is the slot we rest the remaining poles into. Going from right to left in the West Space, either lay in 2 poles about 1½ feet apart for a 17 pole Lodge or 3 poles for a 21 pole Lodge. We use 4 poles total for the 17 pole Lodge and 6 poles total for the 21 pole Lodge. Remember, the largest pole in the entire bundle is the last pole that goes into this West Space with the cover tied to it.

We should now be directly lined up with the doorway across the frame in the back. We leave this space open for the lift pole with the cover for later. So, if you have a 17 pole lodge, lay in 1 more pole 1½ feet to the right of the north tripod pole on the left. If you have a 21 pole lodge, lay in 2 poles still laying them in to the right of the tripod pole. Make sure the pole next to the left tripod pole sits on top of all the other poles in the "V" space.

With every pole but the lift pole in place, grab the frame rope hanging over the south tripod pole. Bring the rope outside the frame, so it is pulled tight. Walk around the lodge frame counterclockwise 4 total times so you would add 4 wraps around all the poles at the apex in the frame. Make sure you whip up the ropes while walking around so the rope wraps as tight as possible. Finish the wrap by bringing the last bit of slack in the rope over to the south pole and spiral the extra down the pole. Finish it off with a half hitch knot and push down on the spiral of rope, so it is tight while it holds the frame.

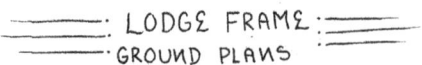

LODGE FRAME:
GROUND PLANS

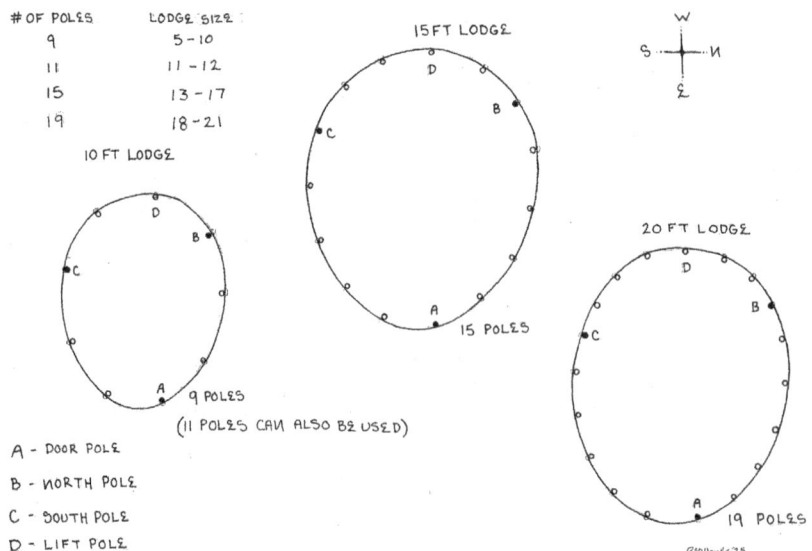

# OF POLES	LODGE SIZE
9	5-10
11	11-12
15	13-17
19	18-21

10 FT LODGE

9 POLES
(11 POLES CAN ALSO BE USED)

15 FT LODGE

15 POLES

20 FT LODGE

19 POLES

A - DOOR POLE
B - NORTH POLE
C - SOUTH POLE
D - LIFT POLE

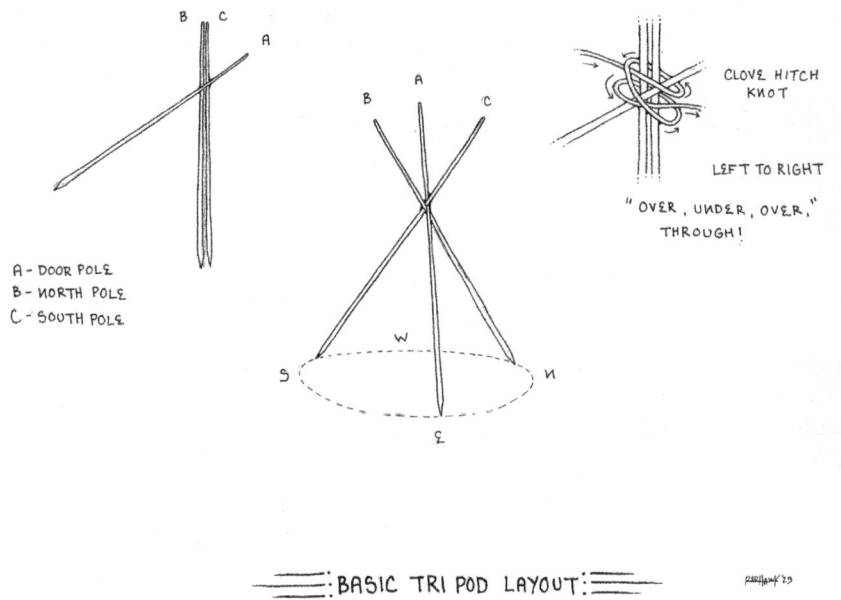

A - DOOR POLE
B - NORTH POLE
C - SOUTH POLE

CLOVE HITCH KNOT

LEFT TO RIGHT
"OVER, UNDER, OVER,"
THROUGH!

BASIC TRI POD LAYOUT

TRIPOD SETUP

ONCE TRIPOD IS SET UP YOU CAN SEE THE THREE SEPARATE SPACES BETWEEN THE POLES ON THE GROUND THAT WILL BE FILLED IN 3 SECTIONS THAT WILL COMPLETE THE FRAME

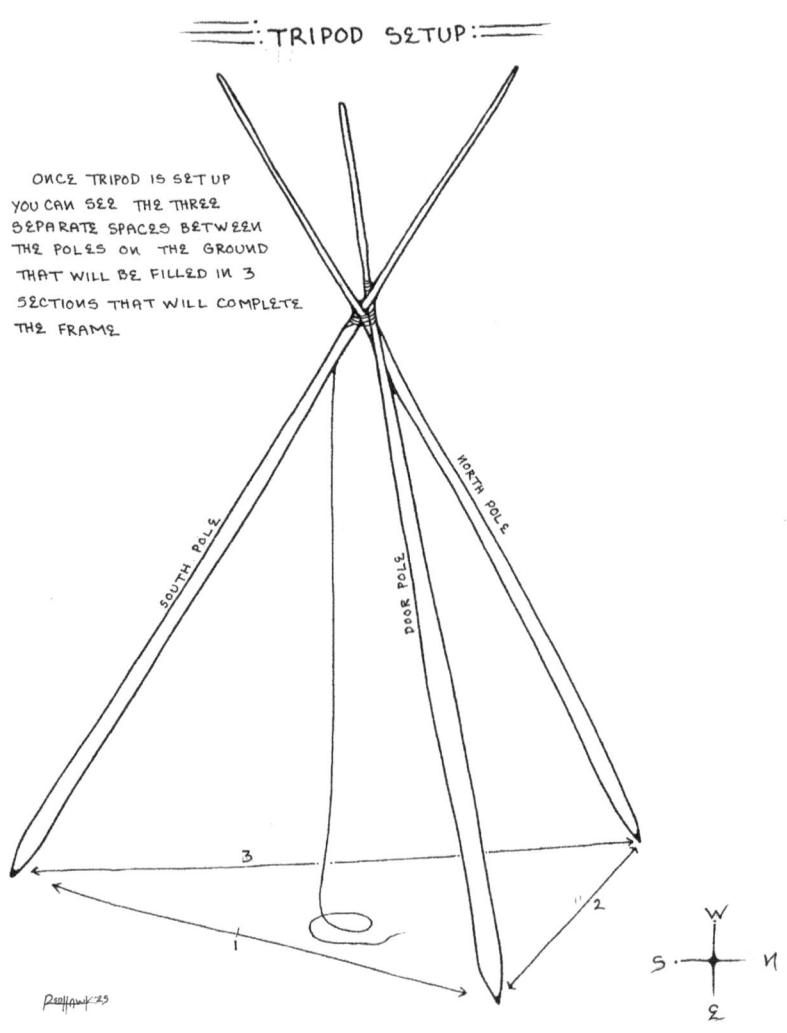

FRAME PART 1

FILLING IN FIRST FRAME SECTION

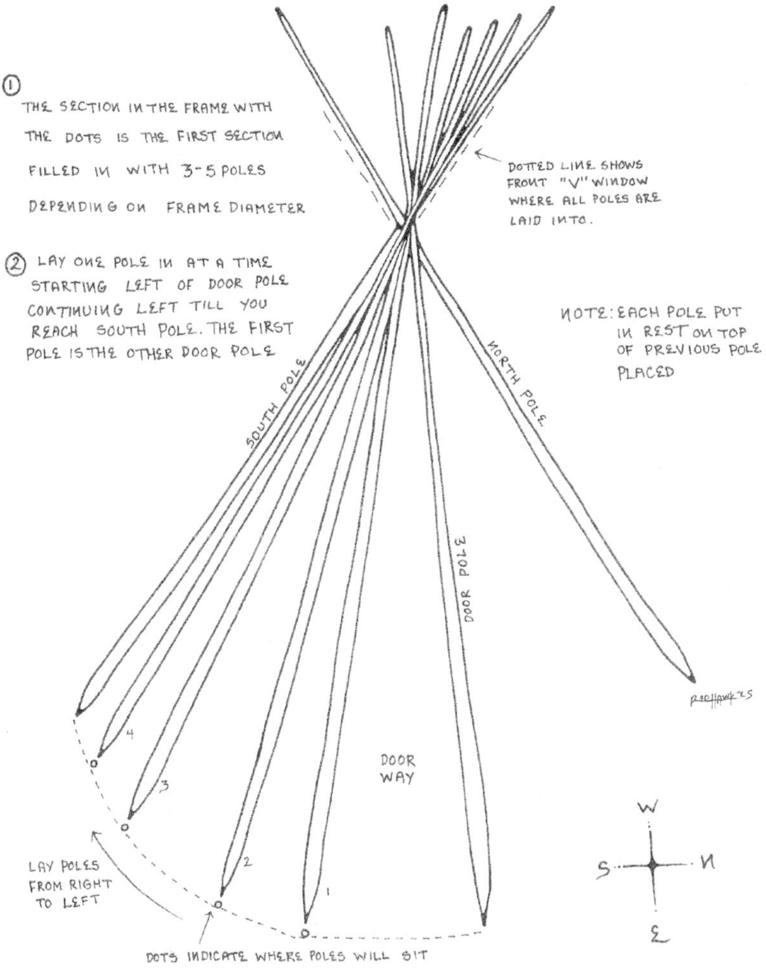

① THE SECTION IN THE FRAME WITH THE DOTS IS THE FIRST SECTION FILLED IN WITH 3-5 POLES DEPENDING ON FRAME DIAMETER

② LAY ONE POLE IN AT A TIME STARTING LEFT OF DOOR POLE CONTINUING LEFT TILL YOU REACH SOUTH POLE. THE FIRST POLE IS THE OTHER DOOR POLE

DOTTED LINE SHOWS FRONT "V" WINDOW WHERE ALL POLES ARE LAID INTO.

NOTE: EACH POLE PUT IN REST ON TOP OF PREVIOUS POLE PLACED

SOUTH POLE

NORTH POLE

DOOR POLE

3 TOP POLE

DOOR WAY

LAY POLES FROM RIGHT TO LEFT

DOTS INDICATE WHERE POLES WILL SIT

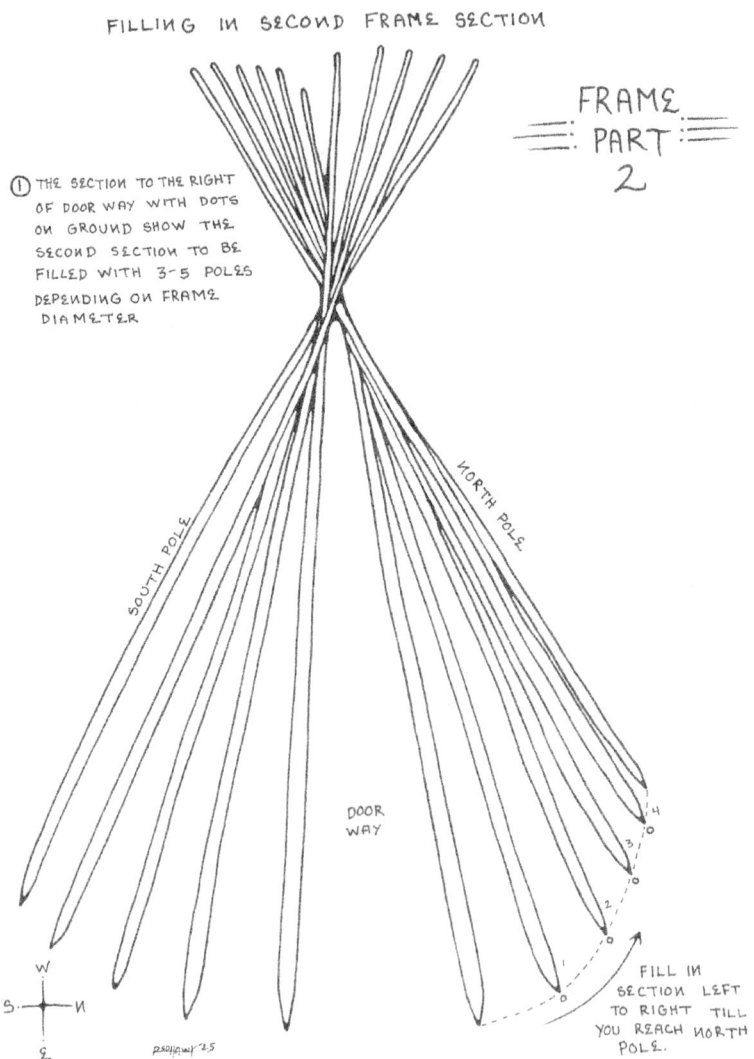

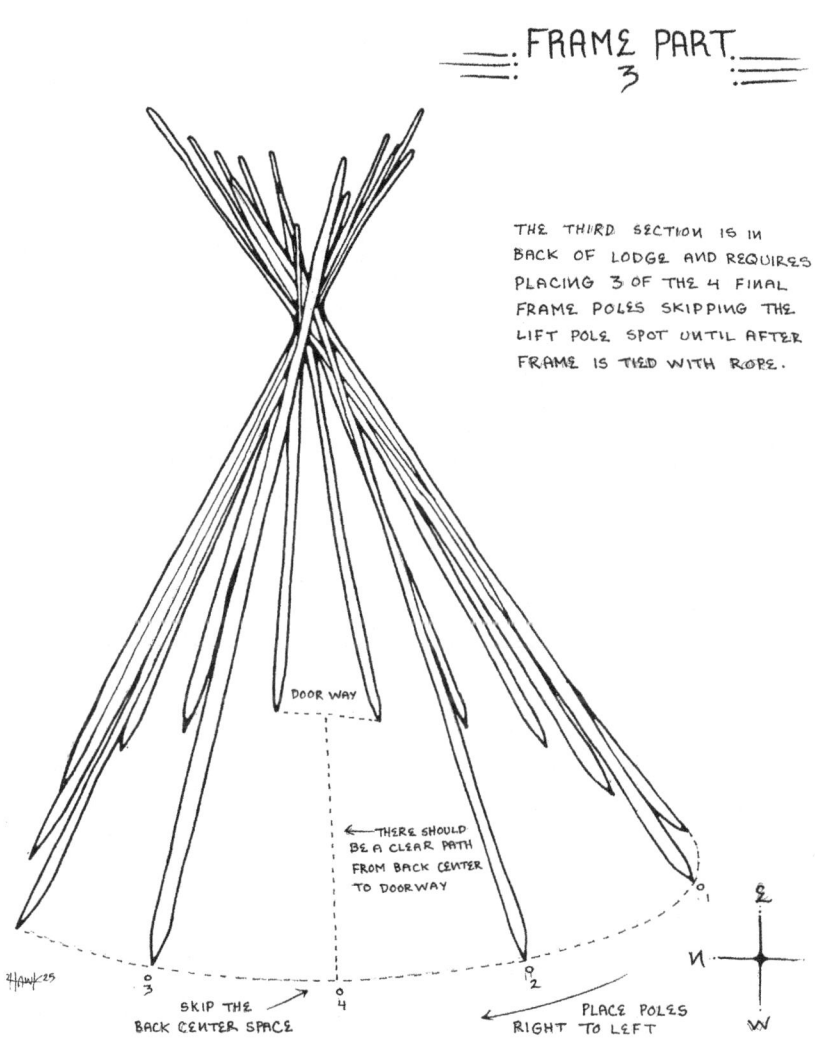

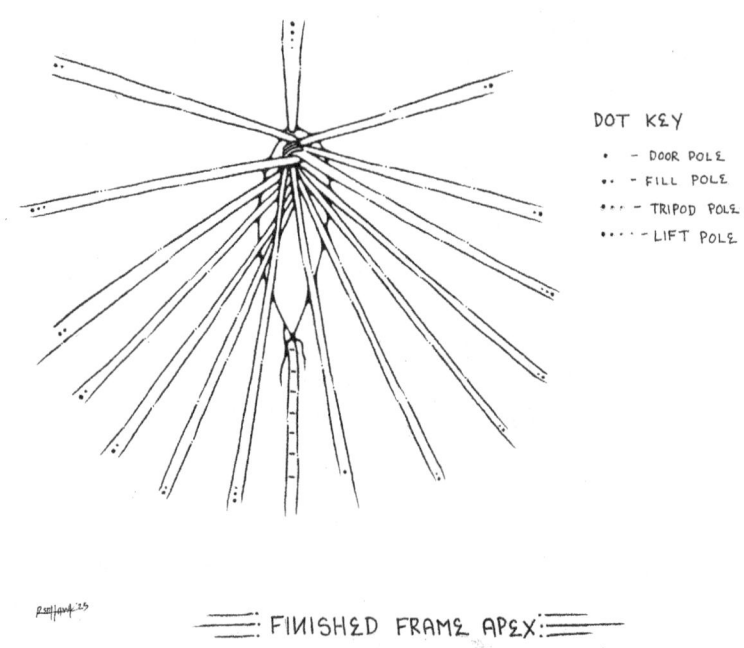

DOT KEY

- • — DOOR POLE
- •• — FILL POLE
- ••• — TRIPOD POLE
- •••• — LIFT POLE

FINISHED FRAME APEX

CHAPTER 19

PUTTING THE COVER ON

Step #1 - Tying the Cover to the Lift Pole

Layout the Lodge cover with the leather reinforcements facing up behind the Lodge frame. Get the lift pole or the biggest pole in the bundle and slide it underneath the cover right in the middle, so the pole sticks out a hand width past the center bottom edge of the cover and the top of the pole is centered between the smoke flaps directly under the tie flap. Wrap the tie tapes that extend off the tie flap around the pole down on the tie flap so they can tie the cover to the pole. Wrap and tie the tie-tapes as tight as you can.

Get a 4-foot piece of cotton cord and wrap it around the pole along the tie flap to add even more security to this tie point. The cover cannot slip 1 inch from the correct tie point on the lift pole, or the cover will not fit the frame properly. Once the lift pole is tied to the cover, roll up each half of the cover toward the center pole, creating a big canvas bundle on the lift pole. Use the smoke flap cords to wrap around the whole bundle so you have a neat package to lift into place on the frame.

Step #2 - Putting the Cover on

From the place right behind the back center of the frame, lift your cover bundle up and slowly place the tip of the lift pole into the small "V" slot in the crown of the poles. Unwrap the smoke flap cords from around the bundle and unroll each side around the frame toward the front or East side. If your frame is measured right, the cover should easily meet in the front between the door poles. You should not have to "stretch" the cover to reach around the frame at this point.

Make sure the tie flap rests on top of the rope wrapped around the apex of the poles. Tie the tie tapes at the bottom of the smoke flaps with a square knot, leaving no gap between the 2 front hems of the cover. Get your lacing pins and start at the top of the front hems, putting them in, going down using the smallest pins at the top, and finishing with the thickest lacing pins at the bottom near the ground. The cover is on!

Step #3 - Putting the Smoke Flap Poles in

We are ready to put the smoke flaps up. We start by getting 2 sticks as long as our hand and as thick as our smallest finger. These are the "holding sticks" that get tied to smoke flap poles. We also need 2 small cotton cords about 2 feet long each. Depending on the size of the Lodge we are pitching, the distance from where we tie the holding sticks varies a little. To measure this first put the smoke flap pole through the hole in a smoke flap, pushing it until the pole is through the hole and stretching it open about 1½ inches in diameter. Check to see where the pole touches the ground directly behind the Lodge. We want the pole butt to land about 1½ to 2 feet away from the butt of the lift pole.

Check to see how tight the smoke flaps are while the smoke flap poles are in this position sitting directly behind the Lodge. When the smoke flaps are tight, and the poles land directly back center of the lodge no more than 2 feet, take note how much of the pole is sticking out past the corner of the smoke flap. At that point, we tie on our holding sticks. Take down the smoke flap poles. Make sure to remember how far the pole went through the smoke flap so you can tie the holding stick on at that point. Wrap each holding stick onto the smoke flap pole with the small cotton cords. Do a crisscross type of wrap to make sure the sticks don't slide around. Put the poles back in place. It's important to have the smoke flap poles in before we stake down the cover to get it as smooth as possible before staking.

Step #4 - Adjusting the Poles

Step inside Grandmother Lodge and check 2 things. First, check to make sure there is no part of the cover touching the ground. If there is, push a pole back a few inches until the cover is about a hand width from the ground. Second, check the spacing between poles. Generally, poles in the North and South sections of the frame are 3 to 3½ feet apart. Poles in the west section are 2 to 2½ feet apart. Adjust almost any pole side to side and eyeball for equal spacing between poles. Make sure the tripod and lift poles do not move from their original locations during adjustment! The cover may still have a loose look and feel, but it should not have big horizontal wrinkles.

Step #5 - Staking down the cover

I always start staking the front of the cover first. With the ends tied together, put a 2-foot cotton cord over the bottom lacing pin. Slide a stake about two-thirds of its total length through the loop cord. Pull the stake toward yourself to tighten the cord. Twist sunwise or clockwise until the cord is completely twisted tight.

Pull the stake straight out and away from the cover, about 4 to 6 inches away from the cover's bottom edge. Angle the stake at a 45-degree angle with the point going toward the Lodge and still pulling the stake toward you. Plant it on the Earth, ready to pound in with a sledgehammer. Pound the stake about two-thirds of the way in the ground or until the whole front of the Lodge is tightened up. Go to the very rear center stake loop where the lift pole sits. Put a stake in twisted sunwise, pull it tight, angled at 45 degrees, and pound down two-thirds its length. This should tighten the entire length of the back of the Lodge. Go around the Lodge staking in on 1 side, then staking down the opposite side until all stakes are in.

Step #6 - Final adjustments

Go inside the Lodge. Start in the back of the Lodge, push each pole (except for the tripod and lifting poles) out until the cover is almost drum-tight and a full hand width off the ground, the entire circumference of the Lodge. Double-check to make sure all poles are evenly spaced apart, generally 3 to 4 feet, depending on the lodge size. Sometimes Earth variations prevent all of the cover from being off the ground, but the goal is to have a ventilation gap all the way around, 2 to 4 inches wide.

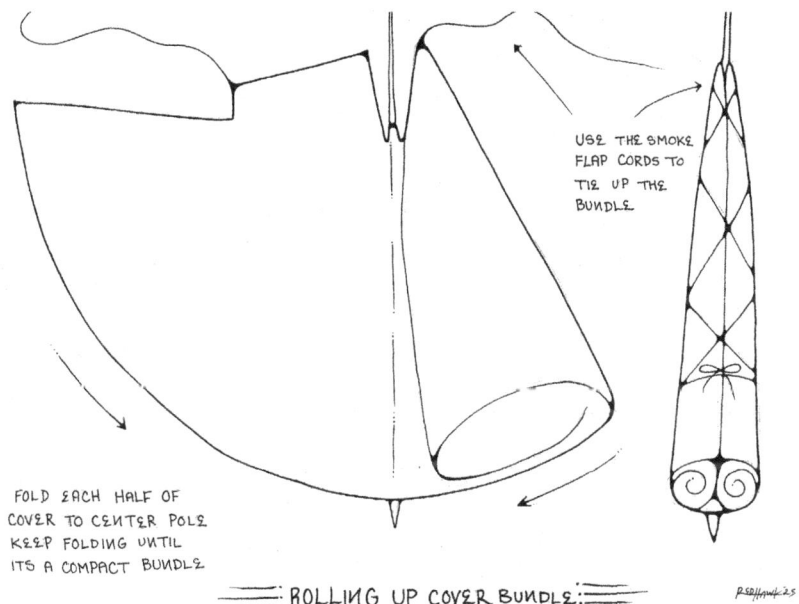

ROLLING UP COVER BUNDLE

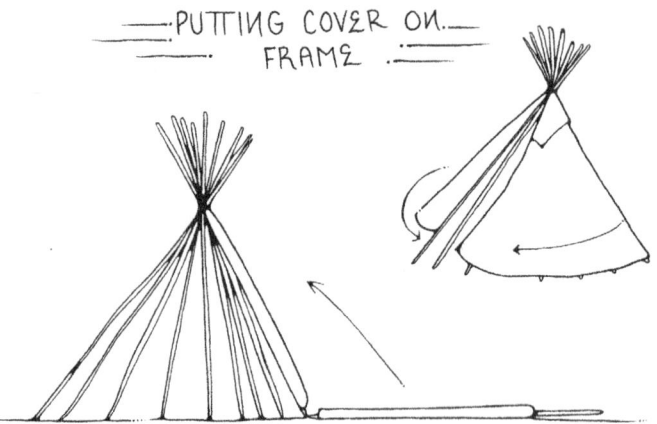

PUTTING COVER ON FRAME

① THE COVER BUNDLE SHOULD BE LAID IN PLACE ON THE GROUND LINED UP WITH THE OPEN SPACE IN THE BACK OF THE FRAME. LIFT BUNDLE SLOWLY INTO PLACE.

② UNTIE THE SMOKE FLAP CORDS AND UNWRAP EACH HALF OF COVER AROUND ITS SIDE OF THE FRAME MEETING BETWEEN THE DOOR POLES.

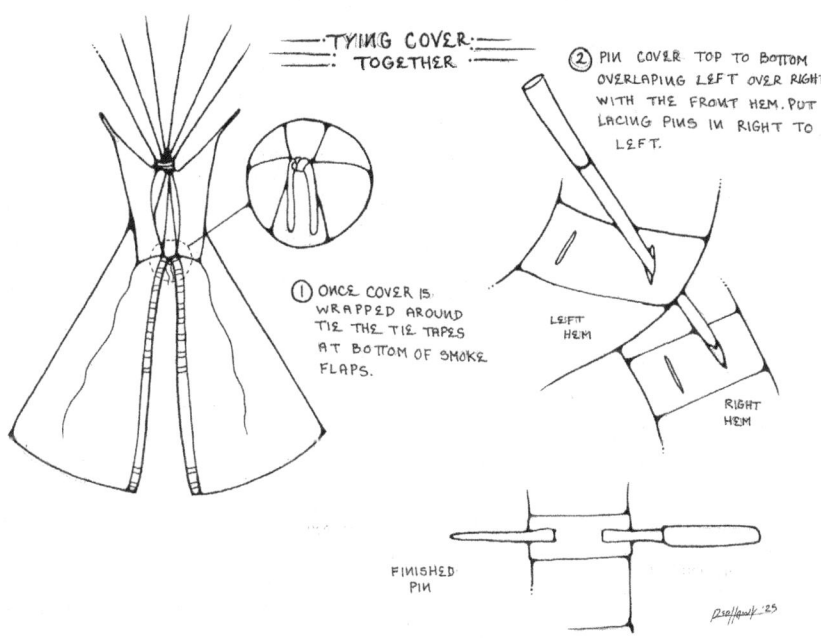

CHAPTER 20

HANGING THE DEW CLOTH

Section 1 - Setting the Rope

Step #1 - Get your ¼ inch sisal rope and find the center of the total length of the rope. Mark this center point with a piece of tape or marker.

Step #2 - Starting inside the Lodge facing the doorway, bring the rope so the center mark lines up between the door poles at the height of the first lacing pin above the doorway. The point is for each half of the rope to go around each side of the Lodge and meet at the lift pole and tie to it at a height that will hang the dew cloth rope 4 inches above the actual dew cloth height. This way, we can untie the rope and remove the lift pole with the cover off of the frame without taking the whole dew cloth down.

Step #3 - Bring each half of the rope and wrap it around its side of the Lodge, wrapping the rope around every pole as you go. Start each wrap around the poles by first wrapping the rope over the front of the pole facing you. Then, tuck it behind and around the pole next to the cover and bring it under the previous portion of the rope. An "over/under" wrap around each pole at about 5½ feet high from the bottom of each pole. Do this to every pole and tie them off around the lift pole in the back center with a square knot. Make sure there is no slack on the rope between the poles, but not so tight that you're pulling the poles out of place.

Step #4 - Get your 30 or 38 rain channel sticks and put 2 under each rope where it crosses in front of the pole, creating an opening to slide one stick to the left and one to the right sides of the front of the pole to create a rain channel for water flow under the rope. Each stick will also tighten up the entire dew cloth rope.

Section 2 - Hanging the Panels

Step #1 - Start by hanging the first section of dew cloth from the middle of the doorway, going left until it's all hung. Make sure you keep the slack pulled out along the rope.

Step #2 - Then hang the second dew cloth panel starting in the middle of the doorway, going right around the Lodge.

Step #3 - Get the third dew cloth section and find the center tie cord at the top of the panel. Tie this center tie cord to the rope on the lift pole in the back center of the lodge. Then bring each half left and right, so the panel overlaps the ends of the first two dew cloth panels. The back panel always overlaps the two side panels.

Section 3 - Weighing down the Dew Cloth

Once all the panels are hung and overlapping, it's time to weigh down the entire dew cloth. My favorite way is to get stones, double the number of your lodge poles, and about the size of cantaloupe melons. Place a stone on the ground contact strip of canvas at the bottom of the dew cloth to pull the panel tight. Put a stone at the base of each pole and one stone in between each pole all the way around. This will usually ensure that the draft is blocked everywhere around the bottom of the cover except for the doorway.

You can also use bedding, extra blankets, and other Lodge essentials for helping to hold your dew cloth down. If you choose to put down a few inches of stone pebbles or shale on the floor of your Lodge, you can push some of the pebbles onto the ground contact cloth to create a good air seal. However, if you're in a moist environment, your contact strip could rot or mold quickly. Some people like to cut pieces of whole firewood about 18 inches long and 4 inches in diameter and lay these around the Lodge on top of the ground contact strip to help seal the draft. These pieces serve as handy backup firewood for long storms and other uses.

The most secure but time-consuming way to tighten down is attaching 5 peg loops to the bottom edge of the main dew cloth panels. The same way you put the stone cotton cord loops on the cover. You want to make sure you place the stone on the inside of the dew cloth just above the top edge of the ground contact strip. This allows for the contact strip to still lay on the ground once the panel is staked down. Place 5 peg loops on each dew cloth panel with the canvas covering the stone facing the cover. From the outside of the Lodge go around and use 10-inch-long, ½ inch diameter stakes for the dew cloth. Pull the stake cords straight down and perpendicular to the way the dew cloth hangs. Don't pull the panel out of place by pulling the cords left or right. Pull them down and a little bit out from under the lodge cover so the stake is in the ground just outside the cover.

Once all the panels have been staked down from the outside, go inside the Lodge and tighten all the cords at the top of the dew cloth. Each panel becomes tight with no folds or wrinkles. The goal here is to achieve several things: first, to get a tight dew cloth that will shed water quickly down and out the Lodge with no hang-ups to drip water onto things inside. Second, a tight dew cloth maximizes the livable space inside the Lodge and makes it feel amazing. Third, the tight dew cloth hung properly and not touching the cover will allow airflow all the way around the dew cloth, which is vital for fires and bringing in continual fresh air. A Lodge should never get stuffy.

Between a tight cover and dew cloth there are channels between the poles for airflow. In the coldest season, you can insulate the Lodge by stuffing grass or other suitable natural material between the poles in every other air channel all the way around the Lodge.

Last, a tight dew cloth provides the Lodge Owner with an excellent canvas on which to paint the dreams, visions, and stories of their lives.

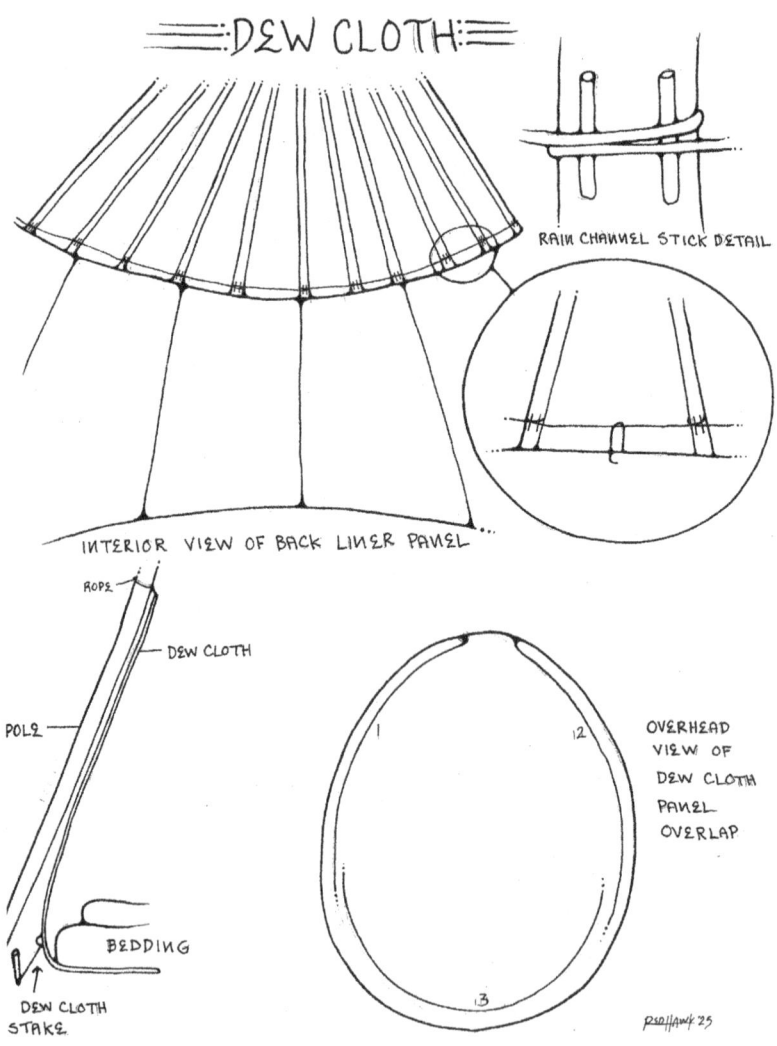

CHAPTER 21

HANGING THE DOOR COVER

A properly hung door cover is the deciding factor in the comfort of a Lodge. When it's hot and breezy out, it's good to just roll up and tie the door to a lacing pin, letting the breeze come in like a guest you'd been waiting for. When it's cold and frosty, make sure a door cover is tied down or at least sealing off all the openings so chilly gusts don't disrupt a fire. If caught in snowfall and the Lodge airflow is cut off, it's a must to use a stick and prop open the door cover to allow airflow while still blocking rain, snow, etc. The door cover is very interactive in Lodge life and requires adjustment daily to meet the needs of the moment.

To hang the door cover, it is best to hang it on the second lacing pin above the opening. Make sure the door cover goes all the way down and covers the opening but doesn't lay on the ground. The air gap under the door is important for airflow and good fire.

If the wind is calm, the ties at the bottom of the door cover can be left untied for easy opening. If there is a wind from the south, tie the bottom left cord to a stake or the right side for a northern wind. Tie the cords together to make a loop that can slip over the nearest stakes and close the door if you're going to be away. There is an instinctual relationship one builds by hanging and setting the door on a Lodge.

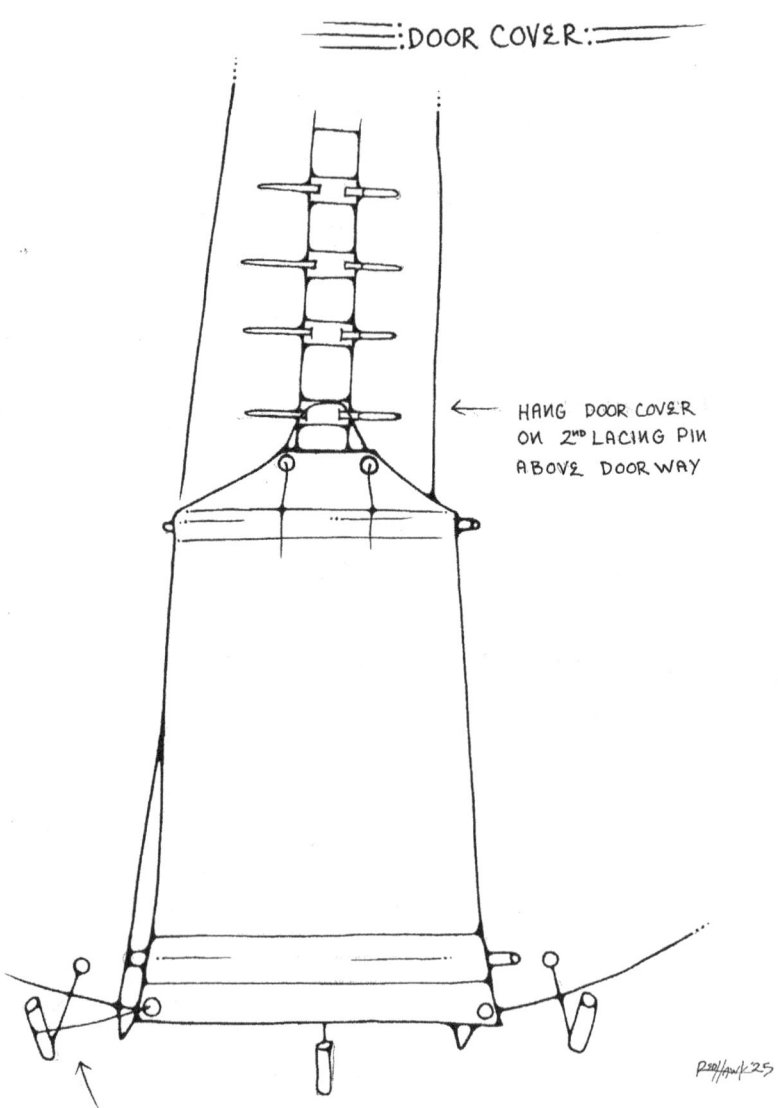

CHAPTER 22

FIREPLACE

Setting the fireplace correctly is one of the most important aspects of Lodge setup. Yet there are many styles of fireplaces, which might be personal preferences. Maybe it's a cooking fire, ceremonial fire, or simply an evening at home. Every fireplace reflects the Lodge owner.

To get started, go inside the Lodge and stand directly under the point where all poles are tied together in the center of the space. Where your feet touch the Earth, place a stone to mark that point. This point is where water drips when the rope saturates in heavy rain, which is normal in all Lodges. The fireplace starts a foot and a half from this point in front of the stone towards the door. Look up and stand in the middle of the Lodge directly under the smoke hole opening. Locate the midway point of the smoke hole and mark the ground with a stone. This stone will be a couple of feet in front of the first stone. The second stone marks the center of the fireplace. A Lodge fireplace is generally a foot and a half wide and can be dug out or simply ringed off with stone on top of the Earth.

From the center of the fireplace, which should be directly under the center point of the smoke hole, measure a foot and a half away from the stone in both directions in front and behind it. This creates a fireplace three feet long and a foot and a half wide, 1½ feet in front of the first stone. Dig this area out, down 3 or 4 inches, for decent coal containment. The soil you dig out for the fireplace should be hand-sifted and saved in a bucket.

This size fireplace gives a fire keeper room to have the small central fire with ample space behind it to push coals building up. As well we make room in front of the fire for the longer feeding sticks used as fuel or a place to pull coal and light a smudge. Every size Lodge and owner will have a different fireplace, small and out of the drip area, with the goal of creating a fire space suitable for the long winter fires with heavy coal buildup, room to cook, dry things out, and so much more.

If the Lodge is going to be up for only a few days, no pit needs to be dug as long as an experienced firekeeper can keep the fire clean and small. An open, flat Earth fire provides the most heat and light of the fireplace styles and can be circled off with stones. Stones don't have to be used, but they hold heat at floor level and create a safer fireplace.

The gap under the lodge cover in the doorway is a crucial air-feeding vent for the lodge fire, and the space between the doorway and the fireplace must always remain clear. This gives the heart of the Lodge the best opportunity to share the warmth, love, and illumination to all in its presence.

CHAPTER 23

EARTH ALTER

The Lodge itself is an altar for the Earth. The fireplace is the altar for the heart of the Sacred Grandmother Lodge, and so the Earth Alter in a Lodge is the altar for the heart of the Lodge Owner, honoring all that they hold sacred and dear.

The Earth that was removed, hand-sifted, and put aside from the fireplace was the first step in creating the personal altar. Continue hand-sifting the soil from the bucket until it's free of stones, sticks, leaves, etc. The goal is pure Earth.

Once cleaned, bring it to the spot just behind the stone that marks where the water drips from the ropes. Using only your hands, make a pile of Earth into a mound so the stone we placed stays just in front of it.

This placement creates a shield from drip splashing in the back section of the Lodge during heavy storms. The mound will help absorb the excess water. However, most of the time, the mound remains dry and can be shaped according to the owners' creativity to serve as a sacred space. This sacred space honors the Earth and is maintained with the reverence of a shrine worthy of your sacred items. One might place their prayer pipe or necklace there. The mound represents humanity's starting point, the emergent point. The Earth Alter is a place to express gratitude to our Ancestors, Creation, and all things dear to our hearts.

≡ FIRE PLACE   EARTH ALTER ≡

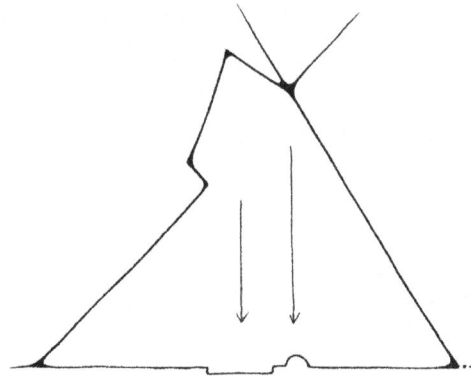

SIDE VIEW OF FIRE PLACE DIRECTLY UNDER CENTER OF
SMOKE HOLE AND EARTH ALTER DIRECTLY UNDER ROPE

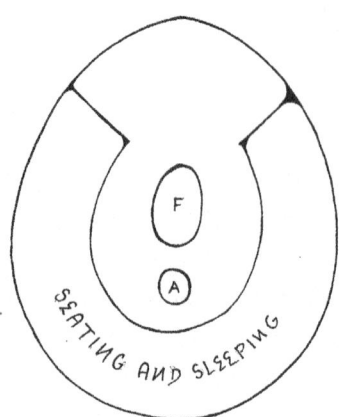

OVERHEAD VIEW OF ALTER AND FIREPLACE

redhawk '25

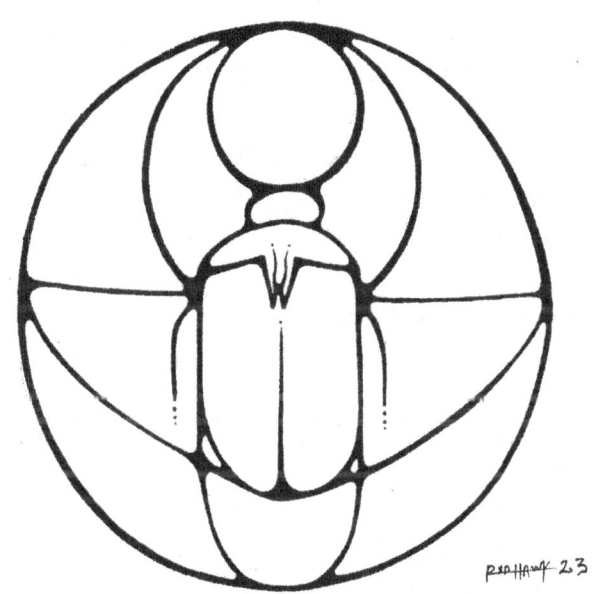

GLOSSARY OF TERMS

Aishat: Divine Mother
Amarukhan: Original Inhabitant of North America
Apex: Highest point of lodge frame where poles are tied
Ba: Selfless energetic aspects of the self, given by a father
Baba: A father
Bayualli: Earths spiritual identity fluid
Celestial body: Any planet, star, moon, or other entity in space
Celestial cycle: Completion of an alignment through the movement of one or more celestial bodies viewed from Earth
Crown: top section of lodge poles that stick out above the lodge and point to the sky
Dekans: 10-day cycle of Earth energies
De Knobbing: Removing small branches and stubs from a branch, log, or tree.
Dew cloth: Inner canvas panels used inside a lodge that air insulates, blocks wind and shadows
Door pole: Poles in a Lodge frame that sit on the right and left sides of the doorway
Drawknife: Sharp blade used to remove bark from wood
Duamutef: One of four children of Heru
Ecliptic cycle: A cycle of alignment between 3 celestial bodies
Geb: Divine Matter
Ground contact strip: Canvas strip at the bottom of a dew cloth that lays on the ground, blocking but not stopping the airflow into the lodge
Ground Plan Measurement: The measurements needed to set up the poles for a frame tripod
Hapi: One of four children of Heru
Harmony: Flow of existence
Hatchet: Sharp tool used to cut wood
Heru: Child of Wsr and Aishat
Holding sticks: Small Sticks tied to the end of the smoke flap poles to prevent slipping in or out of smoke flap holes
Ibi: Heart

GLOSSARY OF TERMS (CON'T)

Imin: One of three Creator Gods known as the hidden one
Jengili: Stone alter used to communicate with the ancestors
Ka: Complete human being without the physical body
Khat: Physical body
Ka'at ibi: Original form of yoga
Khepra: God of divine transformation
Knoun: God of the second part of the trinity of Creator Gods
Lacing pins: Stick used for holding the front of a lodge together
Lift pole: The largest pole of the lodge frame that sits in the back center position and holds the cover on the frame
Lodge: Sacred migratory temple and home of the Amarukhan People of Turtle Island
Mesthi: One of four children of Heru
Nebfest: Wife of Seth
Neter: Male divinity
Neterhent: Divine beings to great to be perceived with the physical limitations of the human being
Netert: Female Divinity
Neteru: Gods/Goddesses
Neterwrr: Divine beings with human-like qualities we can identify with
Nu: Divine Fire
Nwn: Primordial Waters
Phiran: Pharoh
Ptah: God of the first trinity of creator gods
Qebsenuf: One of four children of Heru
Ra: God of the first trinity of creator gods
Radius point: Point from which we measure out and draw the circumference for a lodge cover
Rain channel sticks: Small 4-inch sticks put under the dew cloth rope so rain can travel down the lodge pole unobstructed
Seasonal cycle: A 12-month period from rainy season to rainy season

GLOSSARY OF TERMS (CON'T)

Seth: God of Destruction
Shu: Divine air
Sidereal calendar: Calander based on the 1,461-year cycle between Earth, Sun, and Sirius Star System
Sidereal cycle: A 1,460-year cycle where the Sun eclipses the dialogue between the Earth and the Sirius Star System, creating instability for the Earth
Sisal rope: a rope made from the agave plant
Smoke flap: An adjustable extension around the smoke hole of a lodge to help block the wind and the rain
Square knot: The type of knot used in most parts of lodge setup
Star knowledge: Knowledge of the universe
T-Square: Tool with a 90-degree angle for drawing straight lines on the canvas
Tefnut: Divine moisture
Tie flap: Small canvas flap at the top of the lodge cover where the cover ties to the lift pole during setup
Turtle Island: North America
Wsr: Divine Father
Yennu: Celestial energies
Zamzam: Water fountain in Mecca
Zemzem: Original form of meditation
Zouhet: Selected group of intelligence with its own destiny
ZuDuaNt: Fifth day of the original 10-day week

Eli Jah Redhawk Kenney-Kelley

Made in the USA
Coppell, TX
23 February 2026

72210653R00089